LOW CARB REVOLUTION

COMFORT EATING FOR GOOD HEALTH

ANNIE BELL

Foreword by Dr. Alexander D. Miras, PhD

LOW CARB REVOLUTION

COMFORT EATING FOR GOOD HEALTH

ANNIE BELL

Foreword by Dr. Alexander D. Miras, PhD

Photography by Dan Jones

Illustrations by Sam Wilson

Kyle Books

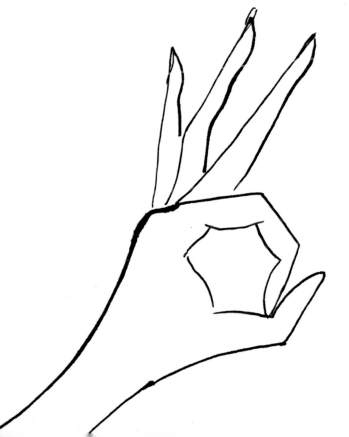

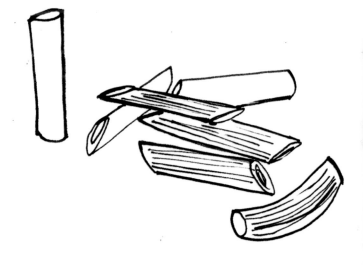

Contents

Foreword by Dr. Alexander D. Miras, PhD

Weight loss through caloric restriction has attracted an enormous interest, both from the public and the "dieting" industry, because of the profound rise in the incidence of obesity in many parts of the globe. Even though dieting works very well in the short term, the longer term results are disappointing, with only a minority actually achieving sustained weight loss. This outcome can be very frustrating for dieters who want to improve their health and well-being. While it is often easy for healthcare professionals to blame the individual for lack of willpower, to date calorie restriction has failed to solve the problem of obesity and its associated diseases. Diet "failure" is almost the natural result of a number of physiological mechanisms resisting fat loss, which is associated with an evolutionary disadvantage. In fact, considering the calorie-dense environment we all live in, our genetics, and the hormonal mechanisms that control our body weight, it is very surprising how up to 20% of dieters do manage to maintain their weight loss, and why even more people aren't obese!

A more successful approach to dieting has been to change the macronutrient composition (i.e., proportion of protein, fat, and carbohydrates) of what we eat. The best available evidence so far tells us that weight loss and/or maintenance can most readily be achieved through the consumption of a diet that is high in protein and low in carbohydrates. What is very interesting is that participants in these clinical research trials were allowed to eat as much as they wished, as long as they got the macronutrient balance right. The reasons as to why diets high in protein can be more effective are not fully clear yet, but additional research has shown that they are particularly good at reducing hunger and increasing fullness.

I was very interested to find that Annie Bell, the author of this book, came to the same conclusion through real-life experiences and research. These experiences provide much needed support to the sometimes sterile findings of a research trial or experiment. Her approach in this book is very different to the previous literature; she has developed recipes that can be readily introduced into daily cooking and adopted as a completely normal way of eating, rather than an uphill struggle. I enjoyed reading the recipes and endorse this novel and exciting approach to eating. I hope that the readers of the book also find the recipes delicious and satisfying, whilst benefiting from better health and overall well-being.

Dr. Alexander D.Miras, PhD
Clinical Lecturer in Metabolic Medicine, Imperial College, London

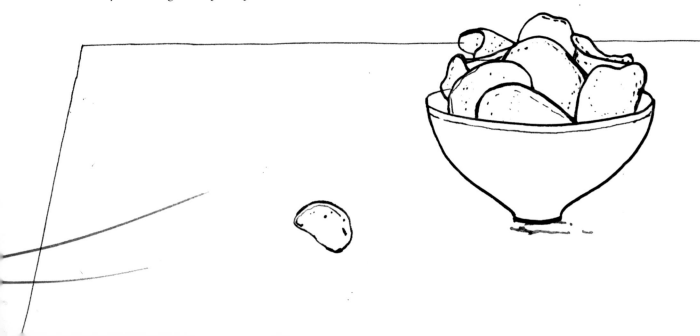

A personal odyssey

When I went through a period of appetite loss a couple of years ago, I had no idea it was the beginning of a long journey that would change the way I look at food and how I eat. At a professional level, for every recipe I devise for salad, I probably devise at least ten for cakes, and as far as diets are concerned, I am more of a voyeur than a participant. So it has been a journey through uncharted territory.

If I travel back to my childhood, I was never a beanpole. My mother saw to it that I carried enough weight to cope with an emergency, even though that never extended beyond a class epidemic of chicken pox. I think, quite simply, she loved to feed us, and I, too, am guilty of this with others. I can still recall with some nostalgia the taste of the spoonful of malt extract that was provided as insurance after breakfast during the winter. But as I'm not someone who can eat whatever I want without consequence, I arrived in my late teens with enough "emergency supplies" to cope not only with my own chicken pox but that of several others as well.

This wasn't a problem. With enough late nights, cigarettes, tangled love affairs, and whatever else, it disappeared. But, as I progressed through my thirties, a couple of children and then my forties, there was an incipient weight gain. Or, as a friend once remarked when *Mad Men* mania swept through the clothing stores, "fashion's made for you this summer." I think she meant it nicely. If I was on the curvy side, I was also quite happy with it. I could see enough pluses, and, as someone who has always suffered from emotional appetite loss, I figured there was, in any case, probably something around the corner that would take care of it. Anything that involved family members and hospitals, and I could guarantee I would be several pounds lighter a few weeks down the line. But, the reality was that as soon as my appetite returned to normal, the weight would start creeping back on again, just as surely as bust follows boom.

Then, however, after one such period of quite severe appetite loss, something changed. The only foods I had been able to face for weeks (or months) on end were roast chicken and vegetable soup, and in small quantities—my idea of comfort food at the time. It wasn't until the end of this episode that it occurred to me that I had inadvertently given up starchy carbohydrates, and by this stage I had actually lost my taste for them. My appetite was up and running again, but my natural inclination was to indulge in lots of roasts and fish, and all my favorite vegetables and seasonal fruits. I also realized that a whole host of niggling discomforts had simply disappeared. I felt better, more energized, satisfied after eating but never overfull, and I could eat any amount without feeling that sense of regret that comes with "I wish I hadn't eaten that." In short, it felt right and natural.

And so I decided to continue eating this way, to ditch the bread, the potatoes, the pasta, and rice that I would once have eaten as an accompaniment and see how it went. Over two years down the line, as well as still loving this way of eating, I continue to be amazed that despite eating heartily—far more than I ever used to and at times more than my husband—my weight hasn't increased by so much as a pound. That constancy gives me huge pleasure, and a sense of security that has come as a surprise. And it left me feeling that if it really is that easy, I ought to be passing it on.

Fashionably low in carbs

If I had inadvertently arrived to worship at the altar of Low Carb, there were any number of others who had gotten there before me. As a means of weight loss, it has hardly been out of the news since Dr. Robert Atkins launched his book *Dr. Atkins' Diet Revolution* in 1972. But for those, like me, who grew up on the receiving end of the government's food pyramid, it still represents a seismic shift in thinking.

The government's proposed ideal diet at the end of the twentieth century had us all stuffed with starchy complex carbohydrates such as pasta, potatoes, and bread, the base of a pyramid, with just a little in the way of protein that occupied the tip, and more or less the same amount of dairy, with fruit and vegetables filling in the middle section. It may have worked for a few, but not many, and in effect supported the carb-heavy popular food culture that exists today, which we now know to be responsible for so much obesity.

Popular food culture could be seen as the pyramid taken to its unhealthiest extreme. Unless you have a very unusual metabolism, there is every chance that you will be setting yourself up for a life of yo-yo diets and "giving up" foods in order to reduce your weight, so that you can get back to the carbs that form the basis of how you eat—until, that is, you are forced to give them up again. But, with every cycle, you are probably gaining more and more weight (Low Cal v. Low Carb, page 10). So although it might taste good at the time, it's a pretty miserable cycle.

Dr. Robert Atkins has since been joined by the South Beach Diet, the Zone Diet, and, most recently, the Dukan Diet. Each of these regimes is very specific and scientifically based, and individually may find fans among those seeking to lose weight quickly. But even without the rigor of such a system, simply reducing your level of carbohydrate intake, be it through avoiding pure sugar or starchy foods, appears to be the easiest and most effective means of maintaining your weight at a desirable level. You don't have to be tackling the extremes of obesity to make use of this system.

What happens when we lose weight?

Low cal v. low carb

When we talk about appetite, we tend to talk in terms of what we "feel" like eating. And psychology certainly comes into it (The Psychology of Hunger, page 11) but, more importantly, there is a puppetmaster inside our brains called the hypothalamus that is pulling the strings via a series of hormones and nerves that control our urges and appetite, hence what and how much we eat, and how much energy we then expend, which together adds up to controlling our weight.

The hypothalmus also receives information about our fat stores and calorie intake through hormones produced by fat cells and the gut. For example leptin, or the "fat" hormone, is produced by fat cells and the more of it, the less hungry you feel. When you lose weight, leptin levels go down and this increases your hunger. Through starving, you also increase the level of ghrelin, the "hunger" hormone produced in the stomach that is normally suppressed by food when you eat. On the flip side, there is less of the "satiety" hormones PYY and GLP-1, which are responsible for making us feel full, and therefore you continue to feel hungry. Effectively, by starving the body, you activate its emergency plan to restore the natural order, which it does by setting aside some fat for a rainy day.

To make matters worse, the hypothalamus, which has been activated by your weight loss, gets in touch with the sympathetic nervous system, which controls your calorie burning, and it alerts the rest of your body to reduce the metabolic rate in order to conserve energy, and therefore calorie burning goes down.

The combination of these short- and long-term hormonal and nerve reactions to reducing the amount that you eat eventually leads you to start regaining any weight you have lost.

"Dieting," says Dr. Alexander D. Miras, "is very effective for weight maintenance, but unfortunately only causes weight loss in the short term." The pattern is that after an initial period of weight loss, due to the complex hormonal reaction just described, your weight will then plateau, and then it will start to rise again.

"Within 1–2 years, the vast majority of people who go on a diet regain the weight they have lost, and some may even end up at a weight higher than one they started with. This is not because we are 'weak' or not disciplined enough, but because evolution has programmed us to either keep our weight the same or gain weight. This has allowed us to survive through famine and war."

And this is where the difference in approaches between Low Calorie and Low Carbohydrate comes in. Dr. Miras has specialized in treating obesity and diabetes as well as conducting clinical trials for five years. "A significant number of patients we see in our clinics are yo-yo dieters," explains Dr. Miras, "and if they are on a low or very low calorie diet, I can almost guarantee that the vast majority will regain more weight in the long term than the amount they have lost."

Compare that with High Protein Low Carb diets, which trials have shown to be more effective than any other form of dieting in both the short and the long term. If there is any weight regain, it is much slower and less than what has been observed in other calorie-reduced diets. In Dr. Miras's experience, "the available data, from studies in which different diets have been compared, tell us that High Protein Low Carb diets offer the best solution to sustainable weight loss and maintenance."

The magic ingredient

The psychology of hunger

I know from personal experience that if I start off the day eating fruit, and yogurt perhaps, I will continue to snack throughout the morning until I eat some protein and get that sensation that translates as "feeling full." It is a very attractive "full"; whereas starchy carbohydrates can leave you feeling weary and bloated, protein leaves you with a sense of being satisfied in a way that is clean and light. It also leaves you feeling full for longer.

But if it feels like that in practice, scientists still don't completely understand why. As Dr. Miras puts it, "certain diets can fool the hypothalamus to reduce hunger while losing weight at the same time, which is where High Protein comes in. We don't understand the mechanism of protein on hunger, but the protein itself reduces hunger and increases fullness more than fat or carbohydrate. With less carbohydrate in the system, the liver produces more ketone bodies, and there is some evidence that these can also fool the hypothalamus, making you less hungry and more full. As a result weight loss and its maintenance are easier."

Perhaps one of the most interesting observations concerns bariatric (weight-loss) surgery. "With a gastric bypass, we don't completely understand why, but patients automatically follow a High Protein Low Carbohydrate diet post-surgery. This has very little to do with advice we give them before this particular type of surgery, but it is also the most effective. It is almost as if it is the patients' hormones and changed anatomy that are now guiding their food choices. This suggests to me that there must be an advantage in consuming diets high in protein and low in carbohydrates."

So there is strong evidence to suggest that if you are seeking to lose weight and to keep it off, the best way to achieve this is through restricting your carbohydrate intake and eating more protein.

If I say the word "diet" and ask you to write down the first five things that come into your mind, then it will probably run something along the lines of "denial," "small portions," "hunger," "bland food," "horrible." I would agree.

Reading about any diet that involves fasting or cutting down, I freeze over simply trying to think through the effect of what it involves. Less food, no food? Giving up? The idea of sitting shivering at my computer, so hungry that I could eat the carpet, fills me with dread.

As sensations go, hunger is one of my least favorite. The yearning for whatever I am being denied overrides what I am doing, to a disproportionate degree, until I can think of nothing else. I am left feeling empty and wanting, a little *triste* perhaps, dreaming of sunny climes and unable to concentrate.

I am not alone in needing to feel full and well fed in order to function properly. We have an inbuilt reward mechanism that acts like a small voice when we have denied ourselves food that tells us we deserve a treat. This kicks in with Low Calorie dieting with a vengeance, making it almost impossible to maintain in the long term. However, with a diet that is high in protein but low in carbohydrates, because you are eating normal quantities of food—and potentially delicious food—that mechanism is kept at bay. Or, as Dr. Miras puts it, "High Protein Low Carb diets work because they are bearable in the long-term; they offer a normal living diet."

Low Calorie diets, in contrast, fly in the face of what is natural. We need to be able to eat as much as we want, without being on a guilt trip or trying to rein in our appetite as if it were a bolting horse, by stopping eating before we are satiated. Restrictive diets as such are not a long-term solution, they're a short-term fix. They're unrealistic, a temporary suspension of normal play.

Back in the kitchen

I was fascinated to discover that there were sound scientific reasons for my own experience. But back in the kitchen, as someone whose life revolves around cooking and eating, I found what was available was lacking. Nearly all the recipes I encountered for avoiding carbohydrates were "diet" recipes, austere and unalluring, and a far cry from the comfort food that I have always loved and associated with family occasions.

Whether you have been on the Dukan Diet, the South Beach, the Atkins, or simply chose to be careful about your carbohydrate intake, you are more or less left stranded in the desert in terms of a normal way of eating on a sustained basis.

And hence *Low Carb Revolution* was born. I wanted to give all our favorite family dishes, as well as popular café and fast-food fare that is so often carb-heavy, a healthy makeover. Here are chapters like Burger Bar, Chop House, The Carving Board, and many other dishes that are a celebration of our traditional comfort foods.

The dishes we grow up with form part of our cultural makeup, carrying with them a whole host of associations. I always derive a sense of comfort and feeling of well-being when I put a Shepherd's Pie on the table or serve a roast with all the sides. Then there are dishes that I recall my mother cooking as a child and that I have continued to cook for my own family. Life without them would be poorer. And come Friday or Saturday night, the craving for fried shrimp or steak and fries might set in, in the same way as a Spanish omelette with salad makes the perfect Sunday night supper before sinking into the sofa to watch a seasonal period drama. I see no reason to give up what we love and are familiar with.

The style of these recipes is no different to any others I have devised over the years—they are intentionally hearty, relaxed, and rustic, designed to be family-friendly and inclusive of other diners. The idea is that you can add the carbs back in as sides in the way of potatoes, bread, rice, or pasta for those who want and maybe also need them. I don't, for instance, need the same level of sustenance as my six foot two teenager, who might have an early morning sports practice followed by a full day at school and then more sports, travel home, and homework. The aim here is very much a way of eating that can be layered to suit the different needs of your various family members.

And it is real food, too—it's not about low-fat sprays and artificial sweeteners. I have simply tried to temper those aspects by using only what is necessary to cook the dish and for it to taste alluring. So there is no gratuitous oil or cream. Is that extra drizzle of oil on the veggies really necessary, or that large spoon of crème fraîche in the center of the soup bowl? In truth, it probably isn't going to make any difference to how good it is to eat; sometimes we are adding a little luxury with such finishing touches, but ultimately the dish is just as good without.

This is the food that I cook and eat every day, because this is the food that I love. Based on seasonal vegetables with herbs and spices, olive oil, and occasionally a little sour cream when called for, and simply grilled and roasted meat and fish. It's food that leaves me feeling satiated but light and clean, and really energized. Consider it a good springboard, for whatever else you might want to add in (courtesy of what I do, I still get to taste chocolate cake five times a day); it serves as a starting point and foundation.

Carb counting

Snacking

I have never personally counted the number of carbs that I eat. The dishes that follow are naturally low in carbohydrates, so simply by choosing these over starchy carbs and sugar, you are radically reducing your intake.

But for those who are on a diet or regime that does require them to be counted, the respective quantities of both carbs and protein have been calculated by a nutritionist. You will also find values for the total carbohydrate and protein content of the dish, when there are optional extras suggested.

There is, however, a fairly widely accepted figure of 100g carbohydrate per day, below which you should lose weight quite rapidly if that is your goal. In terms of weight maintenance, Dr. Christina G. Prechtl (Postdoctoral Researcher and Dietetic Therapist in Obesity, Imperial College London) recommends that you can increase that amount. Equally, you can decrease it if the 100g marker doesn't work for you.

For those who want to explore further the nutrient quality of what they are eating, McCance and Widdowson's *The Composition of Foods* (Royal Society of Chemistry, www.rsc.org), approved by the Food Standards Agency, is the well-regarded authority on the subject, with a comprehensive breakdown of every ingredient.

Bearing in mind the role played by protein, if you are going to snack between meals then it is a good idea to include a little with whatever you are eating.

Dr. Prechtl recommends limiting fruit to two pieces per day (one if you are seeking to lose weight), or even omitting it altogether if you are struggling. That said, the ones to aim for are berries—strawberries, raspberries, blackberries, and blueberries, also plums, guavas, cantaloupe melon, and passionfruit. The ones that are particularly high in carbohydrates and to avoid are bananas, oranges, cherries, and grapes.

Kitchen equipment and suppliers

Nonstick pans

Nonstick frying pans and saucepans come into their own when you are trying to reduce the amount of fat you cook with. Meats such as chicken (with its skin), lamb, and pork all have enough fat within them to forego adding any extra to the pan, providing there is no chance of them sticking. Salmon, too, can be dry-fried.

But such is the delicacy of nonstick pans that even the most expensive will wear out within a year of regular use. So it is wise to buy carefully. The good news, however, is the increasing prevalence of different types of nonstick, and improvements in more traditional coatings, too. So here are a few recommendations:

CERAMIC NONSTICK

I am a huge fan of these ceramic Thermolon-coated nonstick pans that are PTFE-free. Unlike other nonstick pans, which are rarely good for anything once the coating has worn out, these enjoy a second life as an ordinary pan that can be used like a cast-iron enameled pan.
www.green-pan.com

TRADITIONAL NONSTICK

Scanpan's reputation for hard-wearing performance precedes it. I find these Danish pans will perform over a long period of time.
www.scanpancookware.com

For a good traditional nonstick pan, I would recommend Le Creuset's toughened nonstick range that is PFOA-free. The pans themselves are sturdy heavy-gauge forged aluminum, and as well-made as the cast-ironware that we associate with this name.
www.lecreuset.com

Meat thermometer

It took me a long time to embrace a meat thermometer, but they are indispensible in particular for roast beef, pork, and lamb. The Superfast Thermapen lives up to its name, with an accurate digital reading within seconds of being inserted.
www.thermoworks.com

Salad spinner

The OXO Good Grips salad spinner with its pump action and brake is a piece of genius design. Every consideration has been built into this kitchen staple. The mini spinner is perfect for low carb snacking: small enough to fit into the fridge, it washes and dries just enough leaves for 1–2 servings, which keep fresh when stored in the inner basket.
www.oxo.com

Spices

When you move away from enriching food with cream, butter, and cheese, the role played by aromatics becomes ever more crucial to the quality of a dish, whether it is through the addition of fresh herbs, using a good olive oil in a salad, or sourcing the very finest spices.
www.penzeys.com

MIRACLE SOUPS

Soups are miraculous for the comforting nourishment they provide, the way they will sustain you without being overly rich, and the fact that they come loaded with goodness. Had it not been quite so unappetizing, the idea of a cabbage soup that one could live on and lose weight was quite appealing—the Miracle Cabbage Soup Diet. I do recall a trend for it as a teenager, when being able to squeeze into an ever-tighter pair of jeans was such a cherished goal that, yes, a week of soapy cabbage soup was almost worth it. But why cabbage? Pretty much any vegetable soup qualifies here, and this collection is based on low-carb vegetables. I would happily dish these up to friends coming over to supper, and under each basic recipe I have made suggestions for dressing them up, little flourishes, but they are just as good without.

I always try to have a vegetable soup ready in the fridge; I make it once in a while and freeze it in batches. Many can be dipped into cold, but otherwise a small warming bowl in early afternoon is just what you need to take the edge off your hunger. It's a great snack food. So I think soup as a genre deserves its accolade.

Curried chicken and coconut soup

This satisfies the cravings for a chicken curry, and it can also be stretched with rice or noodles for those who want the full experience. I find low- or reduced-fat coconut milk is preferable to the full-fat version in a soup since it strikes a note of luxury without being overly rich.

Serves 6

sea salt
2 lbs free-range chicken thighs
    and drumsticks
2 shallots, peeled, halved, and
    thinly sliced
2 garlic cloves, peeled and finely
    chopped
1 medium-hot green chile, core and
    seeds discarded, and cut into thin
    strips an inch long
1 rounded teaspoon Goan curry
    powder
4½ cups sliced leeks
1 × 14oz can "light" coconut milk
2 tablespoons lime juice
a large handful coarsely chopped
    cilantro, plus extra to serve

Preheat the oven to 350°F. Heat a large cast-iron casserole over medium heat, season the chicken pieces with salt, and brown on either side, then remove them to a bowl. You should be able to do this in a single batch. Add the shallots and cook in the rendered fat for a minute or so, stirring frequently, until softened and lightly colored, then add the garlic and chile and continue to cook briefly until fragrant. Stir in the curry powder and cook for a moment longer. Stir in 2½ cups water, season with salt, then return the chicken to the pan, bring to a boil, cover, and cook in the oven for 1½ hours, stirring in the leeks halfway through.

Remove the chicken pieces and shred the flesh using a knife and fork, discarding the skin and bones. Stir the meat back into the soup base, then add the coconut milk and a little salt and gently reheat, without allowing the soup to boil. Stir in the lime juice and cilantro and serve in warm bowls sprinkled with cilantro.

Carbohydrate 4.2g Protein 26.4g

Broccoli and sun-dried tomato soup

The secret savor here is sun-dried tomato, not an ingredient that we tend to associate with soups, but it provides an added dimension with a lovely piquancy and texture. And, if you happen to be making this soup in the middle of winter, then it will carry with it something of the taste of summer.

Serves 4

2 tablespoons extra virgin olive oil
2 tablespoons unsalted butter
1 onion, peeled and chopped
1¼ cups sun-dried tomatoes in oil, drained and sliced
2 garlic cloves, peeled and finely chopped
a small pinch of red pepper flakes
14oz broccoli, ends trimmed and coarsely sliced
sea salt
4 cups chicken or vegetable stock

Heat the oil and butter in a large saucepan over medium heat and cook the onion for about 5 minutes, stirring frequently until softened, adding the sun-dried tomatoes, garlic, and red pepper flakes halfway through. Add the broccoli and some salt, and cook for another few minutes, again stirring frequently. Pour in the stock, bring to a boil, and simmer over low heat for 10 minutes. Transfer to a food processor and blend the soup to a textured purée. Serve the soup in warm bowls.
Carbohydrate 8.6g Protein 12.4g

WITH PANCETTA
As ever, a drizzle of olive oil finishes this soup off and, even better, some crispy pancetta.

While the soup is cooking, heat the broiler and cook 8 slices **smoked pancetta** or **bacon** on both sides until golden and crisp. Serve a couple of pieces in the center of each bowl of soup.
Carbohydrate 8.6g Protein 18.6g

Cauliflower and mustard seed soup

Cauliflower makes for a beautifully aromatic and silky soup, and I am always amazed at just how little you need to do to this vegetable to reap rewards. It is as though it has been hiding its light under a bushel, and puréeing reveals hidden depths of charm and flavor. Here you have the delicate crunch of mustard seeds, stirred in at the very end.

This one is comparatively virtuous for a creamed soup, since so many come loaded with cream, but here that lovely buttery savor is built into it with the initial glazing. Sometimes, by cooking a vegetable in this fashion, it tastes much richer than it would if you added the same amount of butter or oil at the end.

Serves 4

2 tablespoons unsalted butter
1 tablespoon extra virgin olive oil
2 onions, peeled and chopped
cauliflower florets from 1 medium
    cauliflower
3½ cups chicken or vegetable stock
3 strips of lemon zest, removed with
    a potato peeler
sea salt
2 heaping teaspoons grainy mustard

Heat the butter with the olive oil in a medium saucepan over medium heat and cook the onions for 4–5 minutes, stirring occasionally, until softened and glossy and just starting to color. Add the cauliflower florets and cook for another couple of minutes, again stirring occasionally. Add the stock, lemon zest, and some salt, bring to a boil, cover, and simmer over low heat for 10 minutes.

Discard the strips of lemon zest then purée the soup in batches in a blender and either transfer to a bowl or a clean pan. Stir or whisk in the mustard, taste, and season with a little more salt if necessary. Serve in warm bowls.
Carbohydrate 9.4g Protein 12.1g

WITH HERBS
Drizzle with **extra virgin olive oil** and serve sprinkle with finely chopped **flat-leaf parsley** or snipped **chives**.
Carbohydrate 9.4g Protein 12.1g

Parsley and celeriac soup with poached egg

A poached egg with a runny yolk that oozes into the soup turns an austere bowl into something almost decadent, and parsley and eggs have a particular affinity. But, as ever, you can serve the soup on its own or with a drizzle of oil, if it's not a poached egg kind of occasion and you are craving something simpler.

This is, incidentally, the first outing of celeriac, which you will be seeing a lot of in the coming pages. Apart from being one of my all-time favorites, it is any low carber's best friend in the absence of potatoes. Endless potential.

Serves 6

1½ tablespoons unsalted butter
2 tablespoons extra virgin olive oil
3 large onions, peeled and chopped
2 lb celeriac, trimmed and coarsely chopped
1 cup white wine
6 cups chicken stock
sea salt and freshly ground black pepper
1⅔ cups flat-leaf parsley, leaves and very fine stems

Heat the butter and olive oil in a large saucepan over medium–low heat and cook the onions for 6–7 minutes, stirring occasionally, until glossy and softened, without allowing them to color. Add the celeriac and cook for 1 minute longer, stirring to coat it in the butter, then add the wine and simmer until well reduced. Add the stock and some seasoning, bring to a boil, cover and cook over low heat for 20 minutes or until the celeriac is tender.

Stir in the parsley, submerging it in the liquid, and simmer for 1 minute longer. Purée the soup in batches in a food processor until fairly smooth and flecked with the green of the herb. If necessary, gently reheat and ladle into warm bowls.
Carbohydrate 13.7g Protein 10.1g

WITH POACHED EGG AND PARMESAN
Fill a large saucepan with water and bring it to a boil. Add a good slug of **white wine** or **cider vinegar**. Now turn down the heat and keep the water at a trembling simmer.

Gently stir the water into a whirlpool using a large spoon and drop in 6 **large eggs**, breaking each one into a cup first. After about 2 minutes they will rise to the surface; cook them for another 2 minutes and then remove them using a slotted spoon, trimming off stray tendrils of white against the side of the saucepan. Drop an egg into each bowl of soup, and serve with **extra virgin olive oil** and grated **Parmesan** if wished.
Carbohydrate 13.7g Protein 17.6g

Double celery soup

I've always loved the idea of layering a flavor by using the ingredient in different forms, like a mushroom soup boosted by dried mushrooms, raspberries highlighted with a splash of raspberry eau-de-vie, or apples with Calvados. Here celery and celeriac enhance one another, making a great double act—the sticks provide bite, the roots provide texture. I suppose you could also season it with a suspicion of that elusive vintage spice, celery salt, to travel even farther along the path.

Serves 4

3 tablespoons unsalted butter
1 onion, peeled and chopped
8 inner ribs of celery (from a whole head), trimmed and sliced
2 lbs celeriac, trimmed and cut into 1-inch dice
⅔ cup white wine
3⅓ cups vegetable stock
sea salt and freshly ground black pepper

Melt the butter in a large saucepan over medium–low heat and cook the onion and celery for about 10 minutes, stirring occasionally, until glossy and softened. Add the celeriac and continue to cook for another 10 minutes, again stirring occasionally. Add the wine and simmer until well reduced, then add the vegetable stock and some seasoning. Bring to a boil, cover, and simmer over low heat for 15 minutes. Purée the soup in batches in a blender, and press through a sieve into a clean saucepan. If necessary, reheat the soup, and ladle into warm bowls.
Carbohydrate 12.1g Protein 4.1g

FAIT SIMPLE
Sprinkle with finely chopped **chives, parsley,** or **celery leaves.**
Carbohydrate 12.1g Protein 4.1g

WITH A LITTLE BLUE CHEESE
Blend ½ cup **sour cream** and 1 tablespoon **whole milk** in a small bowl. Swirl the soup with the cream, then sprinkle ¾ cup crumbled **Roquefort** along the length of each swirl, followed by some finely chopped **chives.**
Carbohydrate 13.2g Protein 9.9g

Potage bonne femme

This is one of those soups that I could happily live off and often do, especially when feeling in any way delicate. Usually Potage Bonne Femme includes potatoes but it isn't missing anything without—if anything, it has even more flavor from the additional vegetables. There is also enough butter in this recipe to pass on the cream.

In Normandy, where we have a farmhouse, we have access to the *carottes de Créances*, which are grown beside the sea on the Cotentin peninsula in sandy soil that still coats the fat roots when you buy them. Famed for their sweetness and depth of flavor, they make a truly fabulous soup. If you combine them with the stock from a Thanksgiving turkey, you have something amazing. But at any time of the year, seek out big fat carrots and opt for a homemade stock.

Serves 6

4 cups peeled and sliced carrots
6 leeks, sliced
1 teaspoon fresh thyme leaves, preferably lemon thyme
sea salt and freshly ground black pepper
3 tablespoons salted butter, diced
¾ cup white wine
5 cups chicken or vegetable stock

Combine the carrots and leeks in a large saucepan. Add the thyme and 2 teaspoons of salt, dot with the butter, and pour in the wine.

Bring to a boil, then cover and simmer over medium heat for 8 minutes. Give the vegetables a stir, turn up the heat to high, and cook, uncovered, until all the wine has evaporated. Add the stock, bring to a boil, and simmer for 5 minutes. For a textured soup with a little bite, which is my preference, transfer the contents of the pan in batches to a food processor and reduce to a purée or, if you prefer it smooth, use a blender. Return the soup to the saucepan, reheat, and season with black pepper and a little more salt if necessary. Serve in warm bowls.
Carbohydrate 11g Protein 8g

WITH HERBS
Serve sprinkled with a little chopped **flat-leaf parsley** or **chervil**.
Carbohydrate 11g Protein 8g

Spicy root vegetable soup

Jane Grigson's curried parsnip soup is famously good and has become part of our culinary repertoire. It's a formula to be tinkered with, the combination of sweet and satisfying vegetables with spices can be wheeled out to any other comforting wintery roots, with fewer carbs than parsnips.

Serves 6

3 tablespoons unsalted butter
1 onion, peeled and chopped
2 leeks, trimmed and sliced
14oz rutabaga, skin cut off and chopped
6–7 medium carrots, trimmed, peeled and thickly sliced
sea salt
2 garlic cloves, peeled and finely chopped
1 rounded teaspoon Indonesian curry powder
5 cups chicken or vegetable stock
a squeeze of lemon juice

Melt the butter in a large saucepan over low heat. Add the onion, leeks, rutabaga, and carrots, sprinkle on 1 heaping teaspoon of sea salt, and cook for 30 minutes, stirring frequently to prevent the vegetables coloring, and stirring in the garlic and curry powder a few minutes before the end.

Pour in the stock, bring to a boil, and simmer over low heat for 15 minutes. Purée the soup in batches using a blender, add a squeeze of lemon juice, then taste to check the seasoning. Serve in warm bowls.
Carbohydrate 12g Protein 7.4g

WITH APPLE CHUTNEY
Combine ⅔ cup **plain yogurt**, a peeled and coarsely grated **eating apple**, a heaping tablespoon finely chopped **mint**, and a little **sea salt** in a bowl, cover, and chill until required. This can be made up to a couple of hours in advance. Serve spooned in the center of the soup, sprinkled with a few tiny **mint leaves**.
Carbohydrate 16.3g Protein 9g

Zucchini, watercress, and mint soup

Cooking the zucchini to a deep golden hue brings out the sweetness in this vegetable. It also reduces to a luxuriously silky texture that accounts for the body of the soup, which assumes a rich creaminess that belies its healthy profile. A mass of watercress and fresh mint added at the very end is both sprightly and fresh.

Serves 4

4 tablespoons extra virgin olive oil
3 leeks, trimmed and sliced
5 cups sliced zucchini
⅔ cup white wine
3¾ cups chicken stock
sea salt and freshly ground black
    pepper
4oz watercress
a few mint leaves, plus a little
    finely chopped, to serve

Heat a tablespoon of oil in a large saucepan over medium heat, add the leeks, and cook for about 5 minutes, stirring frequently, until softened and starting to color, then remove to a bowl. You will need to cook the zucchini in batches, so add another tablespoon of oil to the pan and cook about a third of the zucchini for about 5 minutes, stirring frequently, until softened and lightly golden. Transfer these to the bowl with the leeks and cook the remaining zucchini in the same way.

Return all the vegetables to the saucepan, add the wine, and simmer until well reduced, then add the stock and some seasoning, bring to a boil, and simmer for 10 minutes. Add the watercress to the soup and simmer for 1 minute longer, then transfer to a food processor, if necessary in batches, add the mint leaves, and blend to a textured purée. If necessary, gently reheat then ladle into warm bowls and sprinkle with a little finely chopped mint.
Carbohydrate 6.7g Protein 11.1g

WITH YOGURT
Dress this up with a spoonful of **yogurt** before sprinkling with a little finely chopped **mint**.
Carbohydrate 7.9g Protein 12g

Rustic pumpkin vichyssoise

Textured soups are, somehow, particularly comforting and nourishing, perhaps because they give you a sense of eating real food as opposed to simply drinking a liquid. This one has everything you would expect from a vichyssoise (leeks and chicken stock sharpened by a little wine), with pumpkin standing in for the potatoes.

Serves 6

3 tablespoons unsalted butter
5½ cups sliced leeks
1 large onion, peeled and chopped
¾ cup white wine
14oz pumpkin flesh, diced
5 cups fresh chicken or
   vegetable stock
sea salt and freshly ground black
   pepper
2 handfuls coarsely chopped flat-
   leaf parsley, plus extra to serve

Melt the butter in a large saucepan over medium-low heat and cook the leeks and onion for 8–10 minutes, stirring occasionally, until they are silky and soft without coloring. Pour in the wine and reduce until syrupy. Add the pumpkin to the pan, stir it around for a minute, then add the stock and some seasoning. Bring to a boil and simmer for 10 minutes.

Briefly blend the soup in batches in a food processor with the parsley, just enough to break up the vegetables—there should be visible chunks of pumpkin. Return it to a clean saucepan, taste to check the seasoning, and gently reheat. Serve in warm bowls, sprinkled with a little extra parsley.
Carbohydrate 8.9g Protein 8.5g

WITH A FLOURISH
Sprinkle with coarsely chopped **flat-leaf parsley**, with or without a spoon of **low-fat crème fraîche**.
Carbohydrate 10.7g Protein 9.7g

Chilled watermelon and cucumber soup

This is just a little bit pinker and prettier than a classic gazpacho, with watermelon in place of tomatoes. As with the gazpacho on page 30, you can add a teaspoon of sugar.

Serves 4

2 cucumbers, ends discarded, peeled
   and chopped (about 1 lb)
3¼ cups chopped seeded watermelon
1 teaspoon chopped shallot
3 tablespoons lemon juice
¼ cup extra virgin olive oil
1–2 rounded teaspoons sea salt

Purée all the ingredients in a blender, then pass through a sieve into a bowl, cover, and chill for at least a couple of hours.
Carbohydrate 11g Protein 1.5g

WITH CHIVES
Serve with a drizzle of **extra virgin olive oil**, sprinkled with finely chopped **chives**.
Carbohydrate 11g Protein 1.6g

Spinach soup with roasted garlic cream

The deep pea-green of a spinach soup is deliciously dramatic, this one is a mélange of spring onions and watercress. Some crispy lardons and a poached egg (see page 23) would be other good additions, especially in tandem with the garlic cream. Why not?

Serves 4

3 tablespoons extra virgin olive oil
2 bunches of scallions, trimmed and sliced
3⅓ cups chicken stock
sea salt and freshly ground black pepper
1 lb spinach
4 oz watercress

Heat the oil in a large saucepan over medium heat, add the scallions, and cook for 5–7 minutes, stirring occasionally, until softened and glossy without coloring. Add the chicken stock and some seasoning, bring to a boil, and add the spinach in several batches, pushing it down into the liquid to submerge it, along with the watercress. Bring the stock back to a boil, then cover and simmer over low heat for 5 minutes. Purée the soup in batches in a blender. Return to the pan and taste to check the seasoning. If necessary, reheat then serve in warm bowls.
Carbohydrate 4.1g Protein 11.3g

WITH ROASTED GARLIC CREAM
An hour or two in advance of eating, preheat the oven to 225°F and roast a large **head of garlic** for 30 minutes, then set aside until it is cool enough to handle, or leave to cool completely.

Just before eating, squeeze the cloves from the husk into a small saucepan. Add a tablespoon of **extra virgin olive oil**, ⅓ cup **low-fat crème fraîche**, 1 teaspoon of **Madeira** or **medium sherry** if wished, and a pinch of **sea salt**, and simmer for about a minute, mashing the garlic into the cream until it enriches and thickens slightly.

Serve the soup with a swirl of warm garlic cream, and a little more **extra virgin olive oil** drizzled over if wished.
Carbohydrate 7g Protein 13g

Roasted tomato gazpacho

A speedy tomato soup that requires no simmering or chopping—just pop a pan of tomatoes on the vine into a hot oven and you're pretty much there. You could eat it without further ado, but add in a cooling cucumber salsa and you have a gazpacho of sorts. For those not counting carbs, you can also add a teaspoon of sugar to the soup.

Serves 4

3⅓ lbs tomatoes on the vine
5 garlic cloves, unpeeled
6 tablespoons extra virgin olive oil
sea salt and freshly ground black
    pepper
1 teaspoon balsamic vinegar

1 cucumber, peeled, halved and
    seeded, cut into ½-inch dice
1 baby red or yellow pepper, cut
    into ½-inch-long fine strips
1 tablespoon finely chopped red
    onion
1 tablespoon extra virgin olive oil
1 tablespoon lemon or lime juice
sea salt
coarsely chopped cilantro, to serve

Preheat the oven to 475°F. Arrange the tomatoes in a large roasting pan in a single layer with the garlic cloves, drizzle on 3 tablespoons of oil, and roast for 20 minutes. Once they are cool enough to handle, pinch the tomatoes off the vines, squeeze the garlic from its casing, and put these into a blender with any roasting juices. Add a good dose of salt, some black pepper, the vinegar, and the remaining oil, and blend. Pass through a sieve into a bowl, cover, leave to cool, and then chill.
Carbohydrate 12.9g Protein 3.1g

WITH SALSA
You can prepare and combine the vegetables for the salsa in advance, cover, and set aside. Shortly before serving, toss them with the oil, the lemon or lime juice, and some salt. Serve this spooned over the soup, sprinkled with a little cilantro.
Carbohydrate 14.4g Protein 3.6g

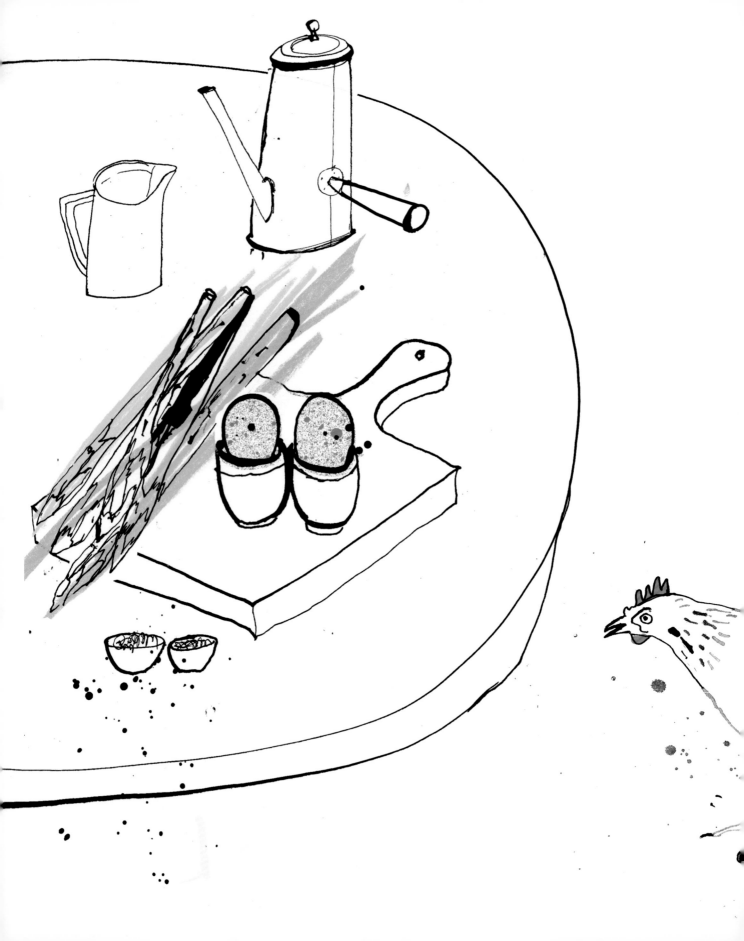

ELEGANT EGGS

Early mornings can present a challenge to those avoiding breakfast cereal, toast, and pastries. And for those who don't have a taste for salmon teriyaki first thing, eggs are the gateway to breakfast nirvana. I am hopeless at the French-style of rolled omelette, and it is much more likely to be a Spanish *revueltos*, also known as a "Chloe Moretz Omelette" in our house on account of a Youtube clip. For this friendly cross between scrambled eggs and an omelette, you fold the cooked ingredient of your choice, such as shreds of ham, fried mushrooms, or diced asparagus, into a couple of seasoned beaten eggs, and scramble in a very hot frying pan with a trickle of olive oil.

Frittatas work wonders for the confidence of the butter-fingered, designed to be eaten cold as well as hot. If you don't have time in the morning, make it the day before and you have suitable grazing on which to start the day. I cannot live without a Spanish tortilla, but all those potatoes—hence the recipe that follows, made with celeriac, which goes beautifully with prosciutto, and olives as the day wears on.

Eggs, too, answer the call for a protein snack throughout the day. This could be quail eggs for dipping into sea salt, or a fried egg with a dash of chile sauce, while mayonnaise turns any *crudité* into a treat, crisp leaves of lettuce heart especially with a sliver of anchovy.

SNACKS

Quail eggs and sea salt

Soft-boiled quail eggs that take up the odd ethereal flake or two of Maldon sea salt when lightly dipped are a favorite snack in this house, sometimes accompanied by olives and pickles. And just in case you are new to quail eggs, there is an art to peeling them—by gently rolling a cooked egg on the surface of the table, which crackles its shell before breaking the membrane and peeling it off with the shell.

Allow about 4 **quail eggs** per person. Bring a pan of water to a boil and gently lower in the quail eggs (if cooking more than a couple of dozen this is easiest done in two batches), and boil for 2½ minutes to leave them wet in the center, or 3 minutes if you prefer them hard-boiled, assuming they weigh in at about half an ounce. (I have been taken aback by the quail eggs in France that are double the size of the ones I am accustomed to cooking.) Drain and refill the pan with cold water to stop the yolk from cooking any further. Have **sea salt** available for serving.
Carbohydrate 0g Protein 7.2g

Fried egg and chile sauce

A slightly louche snack, but ultimately rather healthy, especially if you throw in a few small lettuce leaves. Fried eggs are a great cause for debate—I like to fry the white to a lacy crisp around the edges before flipping the egg momentarily to seal the top of the yolk that remains runny within.

For a snack for one, heat a tablespoon of **peanut** or **vegetable oil** in a nonstick frying pan over medium–high heat. Break in an **egg**, season with **sea salt** and **black pepper,** and cook for about 2 minutes until golden on the underside and the edges look lacy and crisp. Carefully turn with a spatula and cook the yolk side for about 10 seconds, then slip onto a plate and serve with **chile sauce.**
Carbohydrate 0.2g Protein 6.9g

Egg salad cups

You don't have to be avoiding carbs to make small lettuce heart leaves filled with egg salad, one of the best hand-me-rounds or snacks. I wheel these out endlessly at cocktail parties, picnics, teas, any excuse, it's the best part of the sandwich without the bread.

Makes about 24

**3 endive heads, red or green,
    or 2–4 Boston lettuces**

Egg salad:
6 large eggs
4 heaping tablespoons mayonnaise
**sea salt and freshly ground black
    pepper**

Cut the base off the endive heads or lettuces, discard the outer leaves, and separate out the remainder, reserving the small heart for some other use and also any particularly large leaves. You should get about 8 from each head of endive, and 4–8 from lettuce heads.

Boil the eggs for 9–10 minutes in a small pan of water, then drain and refill the pan with cold water and leave them to cool. Shell the eggs, discarding 2 of the whites, and mash the remainder quite finely in a bowl using a fork. Add the mayo and some seasoning and blend. You can make this well in advance, in which case cover and chill it.

Up to an hour or so in advance of eating, drop a teaspoon of the egg salad in the center of each salad leaf.
Carbohydrate 0.6g Protein 1.7g

WITH BACON
Cook 4oz **lardons or bacon pieces** in a large, nonstick frying pan over medium heat until golden, stirring occasionally. Drain them on a double thickness of paper towels and leave to cool.

Sprinkle some finely sliced **scallions** over the egg salad and a few lardons, or if these are particularly chunky, just one.
Carbohydrate 0.6g Protein 2.4g

WITH MUSTARD AND CRESS
Sprinkle the filled leaves with ½ cup **sprouts**, such as **mustard and garden cress**.
Carbohydrate 0.6g Protein 1.7g

Egg wraps

Tortillas are out of bounds, but these wafer-thin omelettes make a fine substitute, and you can roll them up with any of your favorite fillings, from smoked salmon and cream cheese to shredded duck and cucumber. There are two versions, a slightly jazzier spicy one and a plain one that is great for turning out in a matter of minutes.

Serves 4

4 large eggs
1 tablespoon lemon juice
3 heaping tablespoons coarsely
    chopped cilantro leaves
sea salt
1 tablespoon vegetable oil, plus
    extra for the frying pan
1 teaspoon finely chopped fresh
    ginger
1 garlic clove, peeled and finely
    chopped
1 heaping teaspoon finely chopped
    medium-hot green chile

SPICY WRAPS
Whisk the eggs, lemon juice, cilantro, and a little salt in a medium bowl. Heat the tablespoon of oil in a small saucepan over medium heat and cook the ginger, garlic, and chile until the garlic just starts to color, then whisk this into the eggs.

Brush a 9-inch nonstick frying pan with vegetable oil, place over medium heat, and cook a quarter of the egg mixture at a time as if making pancakes. Cook the omelettes for about 1 minute or until dry on the surface, then use a spatula to turn and cook on the other side for another 30–45 seconds. Leave to cool.

– Eat on their own, or serve as an accompaniment to a curry, cut into strips.

– Spread with **low-fat cream cheese**, sprinkle on some **alfalfa**, and roll up.

– Arrange some shredded **roast duck** about a third of the way across the wrap, top with fine strips of **cucumber**, **red pepper**, and **scallion**, and roll up.
Wraps only: Carbohydrate 0.4g Protein 6.6g

PLAIN WRAPS
Whisk together 4 **large eggs**, 1 tablespoon **extra virgin olive oil**, 1 tablespoon **water**, and some **sea salt** and **black pepper**, and cook as above.

– Spread generously with **low-fat cream cheese**, lay a slice of **roast ham** and some **watercress sprigs** or **mustard and cress sprouts**, on top and roll up.

– Spread with **low-fat cream cheese**, lay some sliced **smoked salmon** on top, squeeze on a little **lemon juice**, and grind on some **black pepper**. Sprinkle with some shredded **spinach** leaves and roll up.

– Spread with **black or green tapenade**, arrange some cooked **asparagus spears** in a line about a third of the way across, sprinkle on some quartered **cherry tomatoes**, and roll up.
Wraps only: Carbohydrate 0.3g Protein 6.3g

Smoked salmon and scallion frittata

You could also make this with crabmeat if you have a good supply of it (and this does seem to be getting easier), using a mixture of white and brown meat seasoned with a little salt.

Serves 4

7oz sliced smoked salmon
6 slim scallions, trimmed and
    finely sliced
6 large eggs
juice of ½ lemon, plus ½ teaspoon
    finely grated lemon zest
2 teaspoons finely chopped
    medium-hot red chile
3 tablespoons coarsely chopped
    flat-leaf parsley
2 tablespoons extra virgin olive oil

Cut out any dark flesh from the smoked salmon, halve the slices along the central line, and cut across into strips about an inch wide.

Reserving a tablespoon of the scallions, whisk the eggs with the lemon juice and zest, the chile, the remaining scallions, and parsley in a large bowl, then fold in the smoked salmon, separating the strips.

Place a 9-inch nonstick frying pan with a heatproof handle over medium heat for several minutes and at the same time preheat the broiler. Add a tablespoon of olive oil to the pan, pour in the omelette mixture, evenly distributing the salmon, and cook for 3 minutes. Sprinkle with the reserved scallions and drizzle with another tablespoon of oil, and place the pan under the broiler for 3–4 minutes. I like this best at room temperature.
Carbohydrate 0.5g Protein 22.4g

Goat cheese frittata

Goat cheese frittata is twenty-first-century speak for a cheese omelette, with deliciously crispy edges and gooey pockets of cheese, one for partnering with a tomato salad and a few salad leaves.

Serves 4

8 large eggs
sea salt and freshly ground black
    pepper
5oz medium-mature goat cheese,
    cut into ½-inch dice
2 tablespoons finely chopped chives
2 tablespoons extra virgin olive oil
1 tablespoon unsalted butter

Preheat the oven to 475°F. Whisk the eggs with some seasoning in a bowl, then fold in the goat cheese and chives. Heat the olive oil in a 9-inch frying pan with a heatproof handle over medium heat and, once it is hot, pour in the eggs. Scramble rapidly using a fork for about 30 seconds until they are half set. Remove the pan from the heat, dot the butter over the surface of the frittata, and place in the oven for 5–6 minutes, by which time it should be firm, puffed up and lightly golden.

Serve the frittata in quarters.
Carbohydrate 0.7g Protein 17.5g

WITH HAM
Serve a slice of **honey roast ham** loosely piled at the tip of each wedge.
Carbohydrate 1g Protein 19.9g

Zucchini frittata

Here grilled baby zucchini star in a simple frittata, with basil and Parmesan. If baby ones aren't available, you can use larger ones, but given how easily they grow, it may well be one of those garden vegetables you are able to harvest in miniature.

Serves 4

12oz baby zucchini, ends trimmed
    and halved lengthwise, or two
    medium zucchini, ends
    trimmed and sliced
4 tablespoons extra virgin olive oil
sea salt and freshly ground black
    pepper
6 large eggs
½ cup freshly grated Parmesan,
    plus ¼ cup finely sliced
a large handful of basil leaves,
    torn in half

Heat a ridged grill pan over medium heat for several minutes. Place the zucchini in a large bowl, drizzle with 2 tablespoons of olive oil, add some seasoning, and toss to coat them. If you are using a single grill pan, you will need to cook the zucchini in two batches. Lay them out in a single layer, turn them as they color on the underside, and cook the second side. Transfer them to a plate—they don't have to be completely cool before the next stage, but they can be cooked in advance if wished.

Whisk the eggs in a bowl, then stir in the grated Parmesan, basil leaves, and some seasoning. Fold in the grilled zucchini. Place a 9-inch nonstick frying pan with a heatproof handle over medium heat for several minutes and at the same time preheat the broiler. Add a tablespoon of oil to the pan, pour in the egg and zucchini mixture, and cook for 3 minutes. Sprinkle the Parmesan slices over the top of the omelette, drizzle with another tablespoon of oil, and place under the broiler for 3–4 minutes until golden and puffy at the sides. The frittata can be eaten hot or at room temperature.

Carbohydrate 2.3g Protein 18g

Spinach and prosciutto frittata

This deep spinach omelette is topped with slivers of prosciutto that turn crispy under the broiler.

Serves 4

3–4 tablespoons extra virgin olive oil

3 garlic cloves, peeled and finely chopped

1 lb spinach leaves, washed and dried

sea salt and freshly ground black pepper

4 large eggs

freshly grated nutmeg

4oz reduced-fat cream cheese

4 slices Parma or other air-dried ham, halved into long strips

Heat a tablespoon of oil in a 9-inch nonstick frying pan with a heatproof handle over high heat, add half the garlic, and, once it is sizzling and fragrant, add about a quarter of the spinach. Toss until this collapses a little then add another quarter of spinach. Season and cook until it has wilted. Transfer the spinach to a sieve and press out as much of the liquid as possible, then transfer it to a bowl and prepare the remaining spinach in the same fashion.

Whisk the eggs in a large bowl with a little nutmeg, add the spinach and a little more seasoning, and stir to amalgamate everything.

Preheat the broiler on high, and return the same frying pan in which you cooked the spinach to medium heat. It may already be coated in oil from cooking the spinach, but if not add a tablespoon to the pan, pour in the spinach mixture, and cook for 3 minutes. In the meantime, dot with the cream cheese, then drape with the slices of prosciutto and gently press down to level the cream cheese underneath a little. Drizzle with a tablespoon of oil and place the pan under the broiler for 3–4 minutes. Serve the frittata hot or at room temperature.
Carbohydrate 3.9g Protein 17g

Moussey omelette

This omelette is a low-carb solution to a soufflé, which relies on flour, butter, and more cheese.

Serves 2

5 large egg yolks, and 3 egg whites

sea salt and freshly ground black pepper

¼ cup freshly grated Parmesan

1 tablespoon unsalted butter

Preheat the broiler. Whisk the egg yolks with some seasoning in a large bowl. Stiffly whisk the egg whites using an electric mixer and fold them in two batches into the yolks, including the Parmesan with the final addition. Heat a 9-inch nonstick frying pan over low heat. Add the butter and turn the heat up, then once it foams add the omelette mixture, spreading it out with a spoon. Cook for 1 minute, then place under the broiler for another minute until lightly golden. Loosen the edges, fold the omelette in half, and halve it onto two warmed plates. *Carbohydrate 0.4g Protein 18.6g*

WITH BACON
Just before cooking the omelette, preheat the broiler and cook 4 **slices unsmoked bacon** until crisp on either side.
Carbohydrate 0.4g Protein 24.8g

Simple Spanish tortilla

Spanish omelettes can be made with all sorts of vegetables, but the classic potato and onion tortilla has to be the most comforting. It is hard to guess that this isn't the real thing—it certainly disappears with the same speed—and has the same potential to be dressed up with air-dried ham and olives, or eaten as part of a selection of Mediterranean appetizers.

Serves 4

extra virgin olive oil
1 lb celeriac, skin cut off, cut
    downwards into wedges and
    sliced ¼-inch thick
sea salt and freshly ground black
    pepper
2 onions, peeled, halved and sliced
6 large eggs
1 heaping tablespoon fresh thyme
    leaves, preferably lemon thyme

Heat 2 tablespoons of olive oil in a 9-inch nonstick frying pan with a heatproof handle over medium heat, add the celeriac, and cook for about 5 minutes, turning it now and then until it is coated in the oil. Season with salt, drizzle 2 tablespoons of water over the celeriac, cover the pan with a large lid, and cook over low heat for about 5 minutes until just tender; it may be lightly colored. Using the lid, drain off any excess water and carefully transfer the celeriac to a large bowl.

Wipe out the pan with paper towels, return it to medium heat, add another couple of tablespoons of oil, and cook the onions for 7–12 minutes, stirring frequently, until golden, seasoning them at the end. Mix them into the celeriac.

To cook the omelette, whisk the eggs in a bowl with a little seasoning, then pour them onto the celeriac and onions, and gently stir to combine. Preheat the broiler to high, and return the frying pan in which you cooked the vegetables to medium heat. This may be coated with oil from cooking the onions, but otherwise add a tablespoon of oil to the hot pan, pour in the egg and celeriac mixture, level the surface, and cook for 4 minutes.

Sprinkle the thyme leaves over the top of the omelette, drizzle on another tablespoon of oil, and place under the broiler for about 3 minutes until golden and sizzling, keeping a careful eye on it to make sure it doesn't burn—if it does seem to be coloring too quickly, then move the pan down a little or turn the broiler down. It should still be slightly moist in the center, without being overly runny, but will firm up and cook with the heat of the pan as it cools.
Carbohydrate 8.4g Protein 11.7g

CHOP HOUSE

The pursuit of protein for one or two people provides the perfect excuse to indulge in a lamb chop or a couple of chicken thighs, or to satiate your appetite with a steak. Duck breasts, too, are ideal.

All of these smaller cuts tend to come with their fair share of fat, as does a decent roast, as it is this element that accounts for the succulence of the meat. Without the fat the flesh would be desiccated and unalluring. But just because you cook meat with its fat doesn't mean you have to eat meat with its fat. Once it has performed its task, unless you are particularly partial to it (personally I am not), simply remove it. Your dinner will be all the finer for the role it has played.

Baked chicken and eggplant tagine

A tagine can be a tricky one to eat without lots of flatbread or couscous for mopping up the sauce. That was their raison d'être, to make the most of a humble cut by using it to flavor a sauce that will stretch to feed a multitude of people, coupled with a large pile of bread to spread the pleasure.

That said, some tagines are relatively dry, fish ones in particular, when their charm is as much to do with the souk they conjure up through their scents as with the gravy and bread. This tagine roast is just as at home with salad leaves, ever clean and sprightly, or a tomato salad. It also makes use of those mixed packs of thighs and drumsticks, that can be more economical midweek than a whole bird.

Serves 6

1½ teaspoons ground ginger
1½ teaspoons paprika
½ teaspoon ground cumin
about 20 saffron filaments, ground
extra virgin olive oil
6 free-range chicken thighs
6 free-range chicken drumsticks
3 eggplants, cut into ½-inch thick
    slices, ends discarded
sea salt and freshly ground black
    pepper
3 red onions, peeled, halved, and
    sliced
4oz preserved lemons, thinly
    sliced if baby or chopped if
    large, seeds discarded
coarsely chopped cilantro, to serve

Blend the spices with 3 tablespoons of olive oil in a small bowl, and brush this over the chicken pieces to coat them, placing them in a large bowl as you go. Cover with plastic wrap and chill for at least 1 hour, but preferably several.

Preheat the oven to 400°F. Place a ridged cast-iron grill pan over medium heat. You will need to cook the eggplant slices in batches. Brush one side of as many slices as will fit on the grill pan with olive oil, season, and grill for 2–3 minutes until striped with gold, then brush the top side, turn, and grill this side, too. They should still appear underdone, because they will cook more in the oven. Transfer the slices to a plate as they are ready. Now season the chicken pieces on both sides, and grill for 1–2 minutes on either side to color them—again you will probably need to do this in batches. Toss the onion in a bowl with a couple of tablespoons of olive oil.

Arrange the eggplant, onion and preserved lemons in a couple of baking dishes (about 10 × 15 inches), and nestle the chicken pieces between them, the skin side of the thighs facing upward. Drizzle on a little more oil and roast for 35–40 minutes, gently turning the vegetables halfway through with a spatula, leaving the chicken pieces uppermost. By the end of the cooking time, the vegetables should be golden and sitting in syrupy juices. Served sprinkled with cilantro.
Carbohydrate 9.3g Protein 71.7g

BARBECUED
Barbecue the **chicken pieces** for 20–40 minutes in total. Make up six 10-inch skewers with 2 **eggplants** cut into 1-inch cubes, and 2 **red onions** cut into eight pieces each. Drizzle with some **extra virgin olive oil** to coat them, season with **sea salt** and **black pepper,** and grill for 20–40 minutes in total, on all four sides. Make a relish with 6 tablespoons of chopped **cilantro**, 1 tablespoon of finely chopped **preserved lemon**, and 3 tablespoons of **extra virgin olive oil.**
Carbohydrate 5.4g Protein 25.8g

Baked chicken with red pepper

This is another lovely all-in-one dish, the peppers and onions providing a sweet succulence, so there is no need for any additional sauce. But some pitted olives would be a good addition, or ones stuffed with chile perhaps, and, secretly, I do love those pimento-stuffed green ones.

Serves 6

6 red or orange peppers, core, seeds, and membranes removed
2 onions, peeled, halved, and sliced
8–10 fresh thyme sprigs
2 bay leaves
5 garlic cloves, peeled and sliced
extra virgin olive oil
sea salt and freshly ground black pepper
6 free-range chicken breasts, skin on
1 teaspoon balsamic vinegar

Preheat the oven to 350°F. Quarter the peppers and arrange them, together with the onions, in a crowded single layer in a baking dish or roasting pan (about 10 × 15 inches). Tuck in the herbs and scatter the garlic over them. Drizzle with 4 tablespoons of olive oil and season with salt and pepper. Roast for 40 minutes, stirring halfway through. Toward the end of this time, place a large, nonstick frying pan over medium heat, cut out the tender from the underside of each chicken breast, lightly brush all over with olive oil, season, and sear them until golden on both sides. You will need to do this in batches.

Give the peppers a stir to baste them, and nestle the chicken breasts among them, skin side up. Roast for another 20–25 minutes until the chicken is golden and sizzling and the peppers are singed at the edges. Drip the vinegar over the peppers, vaguely stirring to mix it into the juices, and serve right away.
Carbohydrate 13.8g Protein 41.3g

Roast chicken thighs with orange and cinnamon

The more I cook with sumac, the more in love I fall. A close friend, the food writer Nadeh Saleh, who was brought up in the mountains surrounding Lebanon, tells me it was used in place of lemons in areas where the trees might not flourish. It has to it an elegant sourness in addition to a smoky savor, and its deep-purple hue is exquisite—eggplant with a hint of rust… if only dress fabrics came in the same. It is now quite widely available.

Serves 4

sea salt and freshly ground black
    pepper
8 free-range chicken thighs
3 red onions, peeled, halved, and
    thinly sliced
5–6 bay leaves
2 × 3-inch cinnamon sticks, halved
1 orange, unpeeled, thinly sliced,
    ends discarded
2 tablespoons extra virgin olive oil
powdered sumac

Preheat the oven to 400°F. Heat a large, nonstick frying pan over medium-high heat, season and color the chicken thighs, skin side first. Do this in two batches, pouring out the excess fat in between.

In the meantime combine the onions, bay leaves, cinnamon sticks, and sliced orange in a large baking dish (about 10 × 15 inches). Drizzle on the oil, and tuck in the chicken thighs, skin side up, once they are ready. Lightly dust the chicken skin with sumac and roast for 40 minutes.
Carbohydrate 10.6g Protein 38.4g

Really juicy chicken breasts with garlic spinach

This slightly, or perhaps very, obscure way of cooking chicken breasts is based on the recherché restaurant technique of cooking sous-vide. This is the rustic take on the method, which, when you do it properly, involves a water bath maintained at a temperature a little higher than you might want to bathe in. The idea is that the meat or fish is poached very, very slowly, and then finished in a frying pan, giving you the best of both worlds: an exceptionally tender and succulent interior without sacrificing the crisp outside.

Serves 4

2½ tablespoons extra virgin
    olive oil
1lb spinach, washed and dried
4 free-range chicken breasts, skin on
about 6 cups chicken or
    vegetable stock
sea salt and freshly ground black
    pepper
3 garlic cloves, peeled and finely
    sliced
1–2 teaspoons finely sliced
    medium-hot red chile

Heat a tablespoon of oil in a large frying pan, add a pile of spinach leaves (you will need to cook them in batches), and toss until they wilt. Transfer them to a bowl and proceed with the remainder.

Lay the chicken breasts skin side down on a board, flatten them with your hands, and cut out the white tendon from the underside, if visible.

Bring the stock to a boil in a medium-large saucepan and season with salt. Turn the heat down as low as possible. Immerse the chicken breasts in the stock and cook for 15 minutes, without boiling. Transfer them to a plate and pat dry with paper towels. The stock can be used again: first pour it through a fine sieve, discarding any sediment in the base.

Heat ½ tablespoon of oil in a large frying pan over medium heat, season the chicken breasts well, and cook for several minutes on each side until golden. You may need to do this in batches, or use two pans.

Just before the chicken is ready, heat a tablespoon of oil in another frying pan over medium heat, add the garlic and chile, and cook briefly until fragrant and lightly colored, then stir in the spinach, season with salt, and heat through. Serve the chicken and spinach accompanied by lemon wedges.
Carbohydrate 4.7g Protein 43.6g

Veal chops with sage and lemon

Here you have lots of garlicky butter, lemon juice and sage—delicious with a succulent veal chop. It's a dish for two, but easily doubles up for four if you are happy to have a couple of frying pans on the go. I'd serve some watercress here, or arugula.

Serves 2

2 tablespoons extra virgin olive oil
sea salt and freshly ground black
    pepper
2 veal chops (about 5 ounces each)
2 tablespoons unsalted butter
3 garlic cloves, peeled and smashed
a handful of sage leaves
juice of ½ lemon

Heat the oil in a large, nonstick frying pan over medium heat, season the chops, and cook them for about 3 minutes on one side until nicely colored. Turn them, add the butter and garlic, and cook for a few minutes more, until the meat is nicely caramelized on the outside and with a slight give when pressed. Scatter the sage leaves into the juices a couple of minutes before the end, and pour in the lemon juice just before removing the pan from the heat. Serve the chops with the juices with the sage leaves spooned over them, discarding the garlic.
Carbohydrate 2.1g Protein 28.3g

Lamb chops with cilantro, ginger, and chile

These lamb chops are marinated with a handful of aromatics, and I would suggest serving them with a green salad that includes avocado, which is particularly good with the pink meat of a tender loin chop, cooked medium-rare. Maybe some Tzatziki (see page 81) and roasted veggies (see pages 166–169), too.

Serves 4

Marinade:
4 tablespoons extra virgin olive oil
finely grated zest of 1 lemon, plus
    1 tablespoon juice
3 garlic cloves, peeled and crushed
    to a paste
1 tablespoon finely grated fresh
    ginger
1 heaping teaspoon finely chopped
    medium-hot red chile
1 teaspoon ground coriander

Lamb:
4 × 5–6oz lamb loin chops
sea salt and freshly ground black
    pepper

To serve:
coarsely chopped cilantro leaves
a few dressed baby salad leaves
slivers of avocado

Make a marinade with the olive oil, lemon zest and juice, garlic, ginger, chile, and ground coriander in a large bowl. Add the chops and coat them in the mixture—you can do this up to a couple of hours before eating, in which case cover and chill.

Heat a large nonstick frying pan over medium-high heat, season the chops on both sides, and cook them for about 4 minutes on each side to leave them pink in the center; they should give slightly when pressed without feeling soft. Stand them on their sides to color the fat, then leave to rest for a few minutes in a warm serving dish. Drain off the fat in the pan, add any leftover marinade, and allow it to sizzle off the heat for about 30 seconds, then spoon this over the chops and sprinkle with some cilantro. Serve with a little salad with slivers of avocado.
Carbohydrate 1.4g Protein 22.7g

Lamb steaks with mint and pomegranate

I was a latecomer to leg of lamb steaks, but what a great cut. They remind me of the *côtes de porc* we get in Normandy, an exclusively French cut of pork steak or chop that comes intricately laced with veins of fat and is thinly sliced around an inch thick. I have yet to find an equivalent elsewhere, but lamb steaks will do. This is one of those suppers that can readily be whipped up in that precious half hour between arriving home from work and slumping in front of the TV.

Serves 4

4 tablespoons mint leaves
extra virgin olive oil
seeds of ½ pomegranate and
    2 tablespoons juice*
a squeeze of lemon juice
sea salt and freshly ground black
    pepper
4 leg of lamb steaks (about 5–7oz
    each), 1 inch thick
a few handfuls of arugula leaves

Put the mint leaves in a food processor with 6 tablespoons of olive oil, the pomegranate juice, lemon juice, and some seasoning, and blend to make a textured dressing.

Heat a teaspoon of oil in a large nonstick frying pan over high heat, season the steaks on either side, and cook for 5–6 minutes in total until golden. If they give slightly when pressed without feeling too squishy, they are medium-rare. Then stand them on their sides to color the fat, and remove to a warm plate to rest for a few minutes.

Toss the arugula with olive oil to coat it, and season with a pinch of salt. Place the steaks on plates, drizzle with any of the juices given out while they rested, pile the arugula to the side, sprinkle the pomegranate seeds over the leaves, and drizzle the dressing over both the lamb and the salad.
Carbohydrate 4g Protein 29.9g

---

* *TIP: If you extract the pomegranate seeds working over a bowl, you should collect the necessary juice at the same time.*

Roast lamb chops with watermelon

The idea of roasting watermelon struck me as being on the obscure side of good taste, but I was bowled over when I tried it. The fruit gives out its juices as it roasts, which form the basis for a delicious gravy, and the flesh reduces to a silky sunset orange sliver that you would never recognize as being watermelon.

Serves 4

2 lbs seeded watermelon flesh,
    cut into slim segments and then
    about 2-inch wedges
3 tablespoons salted butter
sea salt and freshly ground black
    pepper
8 × 5-oz lamb loin chops
1 tablespoon white balsamic
    vinegar
a few fresh rosemary needles
1 tablespoon extra virgin olive oil

Preheat the oven to 475°F. Arrange the watermelon in a large roasting pan (about 10 × 15 inches) in a single layer, dot with the butter, and season very lightly. Roast for 35–40 minutes, stirring halfway through; as it cooks it will give out copious juices, a little of which may remain at the end of this time.

Toward the end of the roasting time, heat a large nonstick frying pan over high heat. Season the chops on both sides and sear until nicely golden, including the fat at the edges. You will need to cook these in two batches.

Drizzle the vinegar over the watermelon and give it a stir, loosening it with a spatula. Arrange the chops on top, sprinkle with a few rosemary needles, drizzle on the oil, and return to the oven for 10 minutes. Leave to rest for 5 minutes. There should be a lovely pool of juices to spoon over the lamb and watermelon.
Carbohydrate 18.9g Protein 38.5g

Duck breasts with roast peppers

This way of cooking duck breasts is in line with the method outlined on page 51, and has the same things going for it. It's a great basic, the lean succulence of the meat on par with rare roast beef.

To spice it up, you could also sprinkle ½ teaspoon each of ground cumin and coriander and a hint of cayenne pepper over the fat before cooking the breasts. And the dish can be eaten hot, warm, or at room temperature, whatever suits.

Serves 4

Peppers:
6 long pointed red peppers (about 1½ lbs), core and seeds removed, halved lengthwise and then sliced across
2 red onions, peeled, halved, and sliced
4 tablespoons extra virgin olive oil
sea salt and freshly ground black pepper
1 tablespoon balsamic vinegar
a handful of basil leaves, torn (optional)

Duck breasts:
4 × 5–7oz duck breasts, skin on

Preheat the oven to 400°F. Arrange the peppers and onions in a roasting pan (about 10 × 15 inches). Drizzle on the olive oil, season, and toss, then drizzle on the vinegar. Roast for 1 hour, stirring every 20 minutes, until golden and syrupy. Mix in some basil if wished, leaving the peppers to cool first if serving them at room temperature.

Meanwhile, bring a medium pan of water to a boil and place it over the lowest heat. Score the duck breasts diagonally at 1-inch intervals and wrap each one individually in foil. Immerse them in the hot water, and poach a small breast for 10 minutes and a larger one for 15 minutes to leave them rare, 5 minutes longer than this for medium-rare. Remove the duck breasts from the water, unwrap, and pat them dry.

Heat a large nonstick frying pan over medium-high heat, season the duck breasts well, and cook skin side down for 6–8 minutes until really golden and crisp, pouring off the rendered fat halfway through. Turn and cook the flesh side for 30–60 seconds. Transfer them to a warm plate and leave to rest for 15 minutes, and slice to serve. The breasts should be medium-rare. Serve with the roast peppers.
Carbohydrate 18.2g Protein 27.3g

Baked lamb chops with eggplant, peppers, and mint sauce

This combines lamb chops with mint sauce and roasted Mediterranean vegetables. It's a dish that is relaxed in character. I find it so hard to eat a lamb chop with a knife and fork when the natural thing is to pick it up with your fingers, that only makes it more appealing.

Serves 4

Lamb and vegetables:
2 red peppers, core and seeds removed, and quartered
extra virgin olive oil
sea salt and freshly ground black pepper
2 small eggplants, ends discarded and cut into ½-inch slices
8 small lamb loin chops (about 4oz each)
3 bay leaves

Sauce:
2 teaspoons balsamic vinegar
a pinch of sugar
1 scant teaspoon Dijon mustard
4 tablespoons extra virgin olive oil
2 tablespoons finely chopped mint leaves
2 tablespoons finely chopped basil leaves

Preheat the oven to 400°F. Arrange the peppers in a large roasting pan (about 10 × 15 inches), drizzle with 2 tablespoons of olive oil, season, and roast for 30 minutes.

In the meantime, heat a large, nonstick frying pan over medium-high heat. You will need to cook the eggplant slices in batches. Brush olive oil on both sides of as many slices as will fit into the pan, season just one side, and cook until golden on both sides. Remove to a plate and cook the remainder in the same fashion. Also, season the chops on both sides and color these, too, including the fat at the edges. You will need to cook these in two batches.

To prepare the sauce, whisk the vinegar with the sugar, some seasoning, and the mustard in a small bowl, then whisk in the oil and stir in the herbs.

Once the peppers are cooked, mix in the eggplant slices and bay leaves and lay the chops on top. Roast for 15 minutes, then leave to stand for 5 minutes. Serve the vegetables and chops with the sauce spooned over them.
Carbohydrate 8.4g Protein 39g

Roast duck with beets

There is something about the combination of beets and red onions, and here you have a deliciously syrupy mix where they are cooked in the rendered duck fat and olive oil, with gorgeously pink tender meat.

Serves 4

1½ lbs beets, peeled and cut into thin wedges
extra virgin olive oil
sea salt and freshly ground black pepper
4 red onions, peeled, halved and thinly sliced
6 thick slices fresh ginger
¾ teaspoon five-spice powder
4 duck breasts, skin on
1 tablespoon balsamic vinegar
coarsely chopped flat-leaf parsley, to serve

Preheat the oven to 400°F. Arrange the beets in a large roasting pan (about 10 × 15 inches), pour on 2 tablespoons of olive oil, season, and toss, and cook for 20 minutes.

Scatter the onions and ginger over the beets, drizzle on another couple of tablespoons of oil, season, and give the vegetables a stir, then roast for another 25 minutes.

At the same time, heat a large, nonstick frying pan over high heat. Rub the five-spice powder into the skin of the duck breasts. Season them and cook skin side down for several minutes until golden, then drain off the fat, turn, and briefly sear the flesh side to color it. You will probably need to cook the breasts in two batches, removing them to a plate as you go.

Drizzle the balsamic vinegar over the vegetables and give them a stir, settle the duck breasts skin side up among them, and roast for another 15 minutes. Remove the duck breasts to a cutting board and leave to rest for 5 minutes. Discard the ginger, and tilt the roasting pan to collect the juices in one corner, then spoon off any excess fat, leaving the ruby beet juices behind. Slice the duck breasts, or provide everyone with steak knives. Serve with the vegetables, scattered with parsley.
Carbohydrate 24.4g Protein 26.8g

Minute steaks with grilled asparagus

This is a great way of updating this vegetable: grilled asparagus can be included in all kinds of salads, and with slow-roasted tomatoes. A double act of thick and thin spears provides a little more interest, but you could use either on their own. Don't be put off if you haven't got a ridged grill pan, because a large, nonstick frying pan will do.

Minute steaks make a little go a long way and, true to their name, they are cooked in just that amount of time.

Serves 4

14oz finger-thick and fine
    asparagus spears (trimmed
    weight)
2 × 8oz rump steaks, cut about
    an inch thick
extra virgin olive oil
sea salt and freshly ground black
    pepper

Bring a large pan of salted water to a boil. Add the finger-thick asparagus spears and cook for 1 minute, then add the fine spears and cook for another 2 minutes. Drain them in a colander, pass under cold running water, then set aside.

Slice each steak into two thin steaks, then beat them with a rolling pin until they are very thin. Don't worry if the seams of fat cause them to come apart into smaller steaks.

Heat a ridged cast-iron grill pan over high heat. Brush the steaks with oil and season on either side, then grill them in batches for 30 seconds on each side for medium-rare, or 45–60 seconds if you prefer them medium, pressing down with a spatula to help brand the steaks with stripes. Transfer them to a warm plate and cover with foil to keep warm. Turn the heat down to medium. Toss the asparagus in a large bowl with a couple of tablespoons of oil and some seasoning, and grill in a couple of batches for 2–3 minutes each side until golden, transferring them to the plate with the steak. Serve the steaks with the asparagus spears.
Carbohydrate 2.3g Protein 27.5g

WITH CHEAT'S BEARNAISE
Combine ¼ cup **mayonnaise**, ¼ cup **sour cream**, ¼ cup **fat-free Greek yogurt**, and 2 heaping teaspoons finely chopped **fresh tarragon** in a small bowl, and season with **sea salt** if necessary. Accompany the steak and the asparagus with the sauce, sprinkling on a few tarragon leaves.
Carbohydrate 3.6g Protein 29.3g

BURGER BAR

I recall swelling with pride the day my eight-year-old told me he hated McDonald's. This wasn't entirely without encouragement from me, but I certainly didn't throw a hissy fit at the idea of the occasional Happy Meal when he was young, as long as he could find someone else to take him. Of the many reasons to resent this fast-food chain, the one that is uppermost for me, is the way that the food corrupts the palate. The mushy buns and insidious fat-soaked sticks that go by the name of fries are such a far cry from real food that if you do happen to take to them, then it is likely that the same articles made from scratch using quality ingredients will start to seem like second best to the ersatz thing. Hence a junk-food habit is formed.

When we talk about the obesity epidemic being linked to the rise of fructose or added sugar in processed foods, in lay terms you could translate this to mean that many of today's convenience savory foods are effectively sweet foods with added salt. Take the cheese out of the cheese puff-pastry twist in the supermarket bakery and you are left with a sweetened brioche that would be more at home spread with jam. But it is balanced with enough salt to disguise it. To take account of this increase in the sweetness of savory foods, with everything being relative, sweet foods are becoming ever more saccharine—some almost aggressively so—it is hard to imagine how distorted the palate must be in order to genuinely find them attractive. But to help us along, manufacturers add salt to disguise or offset the sweetness, at levels that you would simply never add to home-cooked food.

Much of what lies in this chapter has fallen into the hands of large fast-food chains and been corrupted in the process—be it fried chicken, burgers, or skewers. The homemade versions are delicious in their own right, if completely different, and perfectly healthy, especially if you cut out the gratuitous carbs that tend to come with them and opt for some salad, or, at least, a healthier take on the fries (see pages 148, 163 and 164).

As for the recipes that follow, don't frown too severely on fat. I find that sausages and ground meat marketed as having highly reduced levels of fat, 5 percent for instance, don't cook up well. The ground meat is inherently tough and the sausages joyless. It is very much at the heart of this book to keep such considerations in perspective, hence the inclusion of recipes for cuts like pork shoulder, for lamb, for chicken WITH the skin, and so forth. Once you start stripping meat of every ounce of fat, you start venturing into joyless diet territory. And, thankfully, fat is no longer considered to be the baddie it once was. So aim for a happy medium; ten percent fat for ground meat should give you the succulence you are seeking without making a greasy or unhealthy dish.

Classic hamburgers

There are very few of us who aren't enticed by the scent of a thick burger grilling over charcoal, the odd hiss as the juices drip onto the red-hot coals. And the best are no more than very good beef, chopped shallot, and some salt and pepper. If possible always try and buy your ground beef from a butcher who can tell you which cuts have gone into it, if you wish to know.

Given how well they freeze, I frequently make a double batch of these burgers so that they are ready for some easy suppers, since they defrost in no time. Here lettuce leaves play the part of a bun, a quantum leap of imagination for some, but other classic garnishes are all present and correct, and it's easy enough to have some buns or pita for those who want. Personally, I love the lettuce sandwich; a crisp green leaf is exactly what that juicy burger needs.

Serves 4

Burgers:
1 lb lean ground beef
1 tablespoon finely chopped
    shallots
sea salt and freshly ground black
    pepper
8 small Romaine leaves, to serve

Garnishes:
mustard
ketchup
½ beefsteak tomato, core removed
    and sliced
½ red onion, peeled, halved, and
    thinly sliced
8 pickles, sliced

Mix together the ground beef, shallots, and seasoning in a bowl. For an especially professional finish to your burgers, shape the beef, a quarter at a time, inside a 4-inch pastry cutter with straight edges. Or, if you are happy with something more rustic, form the meat into balls using your hands, and then flatten these between your palms. Bear in mind that the burgers will shrink and fatten when you grill them. If you want, you can make them in advance then cover and chill them.

Either place a ridged cast-iron grill pan or a large, dry frying pan over medium-low heat, and cook the burgers for 4–5 minutes on each side. Place each burger within one of the lettuce leaves, smear on some mustard and a little ketchup. Next place a slice of tomato on top and season, then add some sliced onion and pickles, and close with a second leaf for eating in your hands.
Carbohydrate 3.3g Protein 25.6g

Gratin of meatballs with plum tomatoes

Here meatballs are smothered in a chunky tomato sauce made with plum tomatoes. It makes for the easiest possible ragù since it's baked in the oven. If you like, you can add an egg to the meatball mixture, to help them hold together. Fresh oregano and marjoram can be used in place of thyme.

Now the trend for sliders—meatballs served in mini buns—has taken off. Baby burgers, what is there not to like? So you could also serve a supply of supple green leaves that can be rolled around a meatball and some of the sauce for eating in your hands.

Serves 4

Meatballs:
4 tablespoons extra virgin olive oil
1 onion, peeled and finely chopped
4oz unsmoked bacon, finely diced
3 tablespoons fresh thyme leaves
1½ lbs lean ground beef
sea salt and freshly ground black pepper

Tomato sauce:
2 lbs plum tomatoes
3 tablespoons tomato paste
2 garlic cloves, peeled and finely chopped
1 dried red chile, finely chopped
freshly grated Parmesan to serve (optional)

For the meatballs, heat 2 tablespoons of olive oil in a large frying pan over medium-low heat, add the onion and bacon, and cook gently for about 5 minutes, stirring occasionally until soft and cooked through, adding 2 tablespoons of the thyme a couple of minutes before the end. Transfer the contents of the pan to a large bowl and leave to cool. Add the beef and some seasoning to the bowl and work together using a spoon. Shape the mixture into balls the size of a large walnut and set aside on a couple of plates.

To make the tomato sauce, bring a large pan of water to a boil and cut out the core from the top of each tomato. Plunge the tomatoes into the boiling water for 20 seconds and then into a bowl of cold water. Remove them and slip off the skins, then halve and chop them. Place the tomatoes in a bowl and combine with the tomato paste, a tablespoon of olive oil, the garlic, chile, and some seasoning. Both the sauce and meatballs can be made in advance, in which case cover and chill them.

Heat a large, nonstick frying pan over medium heat, add half the meatballs, and brown them on all sides. Transfer them to a shallow ovenproof or gratin dish that holds them in a single layer with a little space between each one. Scrape the pan clean of any fat and chopped onion, and cook the remainder in the same fashion. Spoon the sauce over and between the meatballs.

Preheat the oven to 400°F. Sprinkle on the remaining thyme, and drizzle another tablespoon of olive oil over the meatballs, and bake for 40–45 minutes until the tomatoes on the top have started to singe at the tips. Serve with a bowl of Parmesan on the table to scatter over if wished.
Carbohydrate 13g Protein 45.3g

WITH BASIL PURÉE
You can also serve these with a drizzle of basil purée, made by blending 2 cups of **basil leaves** and a small peeled **garlic clove** in a food processor until finely chopped, then gradually adding 4 tablespoons of **extra virgin olive oil**. Season to taste with **sea salt** and a squeeze of **lemon juice**.
Carbohydrate 13.8g Protein 45.8g

Middle Eastern lamb burgers

The four spices cumin, coriander, cinnamon, and allspice capture the scent of the Middle East; an unlikely quartet, since individually they have such different characters, but together they make a charming mismatch. With fresh cilantro, parsley, and some olives, these are jazzier than the previous Classic hamburgers (page 66). And you still get to eat them between lettuce leaves.

Serves 4

Burgers:
1 lb lean ground lamb
1 tablespoon finely chopped shallots
2 garlic cloves, peeled and finely
    chopped
2 teaspoons ground cumin
1 teaspoon ground coriander
1 teaspoon ground cinnamon
¼ teaspoon ground allspice
sea salt and freshly ground black
    pepper
8 small Romaine leaves, to serve

Garnishes:
1 beefsteak tomato, core removed
    and sliced
1 large handful of cilantro sprigs
1 large handful of flat-leaf parsley
    sprigs
6–8 black olives, pitted and halved
a squeeze of lemon juice

Blend together the lamb, shallots, garlic, spices, and seasoning in a bowl. For an especially professional finish to your burgers, shape the meat a quarter at a time inside a 4-inch pastry cutter with straight edges. Or, if you are happy with something more rustic, form the meat into balls using your hands, and then flatten these between your palms. Bear in mind that the burgers will shrink and fatten when you grill them. If you want you can make them in advance, then cover and chill them.

Either place a ridged cast-iron grill pan over medium-low heat or preheat a conventional grill to high, and cook the burgers for 4–5 minutes each side. Place each burger within one of the lettuce leaves, place a slice of tomato on top, then some herb sprigs and olives, and squeeze on a little lemon juice, and close with a second leaf for eating in your hands.
Carbohydrate 4g Protein 22.5g

BARBECUED
Burgers are always great barbecued, in which case cook them over hot coals for 15–20 minutes in total. If you press down on them using a spatula, you will also encourage the branding of stripes.

A trio of ragùs

Each of these has a different cultural identity, but they are all similar in style and adaptability. I am happy to eat them with a big salad, or with some roasted vegetables—peppers, eggplant, and zucchini are all lovely (see pages 166–169). But it's easy enough to cook pasta, rice, tortillas, or whatever others might like. Ideally use ground beef with about 10 percent fat, and if it also announces its pedigree, then so much the better. Equally, buy the best ground lamb available or visit the butcher.

SPAGHETTI BOLOGNESE
This suppertime staple gets wheeled out in our house with embarrassing regularity. And no matter how much I cook, it never goes to waste. Not so long ago, we were having a Christmas cocktail party, and my husband was concerned about providing for the possibility of any stragglers, whom he numbered at a possible thirty, while I felt this was highly unlikely. But once the seed of doubt had been sown, it remained a niggling worry. So, we agreed that I would cater for the "drinks eats", and he would take care of anything required afterward. He opted for Spaghetti Bolognese.

Serves 6

2 tablespoons unsalted butter
1 tablespoon extra virgin olive oil
1 onion, peeled and finely chopped
2 slim carrots, trimmed, peeled, and thinly sliced
1 rib of celery, thinly sliced
2 tablespoons fresh oregano or marjoram leaves, or 1 teaspoon dried
4 garlic cloves, peeled and finely chopped
1¾ lbs lean ground beef
⅔ cup red wine
1 × 14oz can chopped tomatoes
1 tablespoon tomato paste
⅔ cup chicken or beef stock
1 small dried red chile, crumbled
sea salt
3 tablespoons freshly grated Parmesan, plus extra to serve (optional)
freshly grated nutmeg

Heat the butter and the olive oil in a medium saucepan over medium heat, and cook the onion, carrots, celery, and fresh oregano or marjoram for about 10 minutes, stirring frequently, until softened and glossy, adding the garlic just before the end. Add the beef, turn up the heat, and cook, stirring frequently, until the meat changes color. Add the wine, tomatoes, paste, stock, chile, and oregano if using dried, and season with a little salt. Bring to a boil, then simmer over low heat for 1 hour, stirring now and again. There should still be enough juices at the end to moisten a pile of spaghetti (should that be the call), so if necessary cover it toward the end. Skim off any excess fat, stir in 3 tablespoons of Parmesan if including, and season with nutmeg. Serve the Bolognese sauce with a shower of Parmesan if wished, and a grinding of black pepper.
Carbohydrate 6.1g Protein 28g

CHEAT'S SPAGHETTI BOLOGNESE

Here a jar of good ragù will provide the character normally built in by chopped vegetables and a can of tomatoes. Go for an established Italian name such as Bertolli or Sacla, both of them old hands that know what they're doing.

Serves 6

Gently cook 1 finely chopped **onion** in 2 tablespoons **extra virgin olive oil** in a medium saucepan for about 5 minutes until softened and lightly colored. Add 1¾ lbs lean **ground beef**, turn up the heat, and continue to cook until the meat changes color, stirring occasionally. Add 1 tablespoon **fresh thyme leaves**, 14oz jar of **ragù**, ⅔ cup **white wine**, ⅔ cup **chicken** or **beef stock**, and some **sea salt**. Bring to a boil and simmer for 1 hour. Season with **nutmeg**.

Carbohydrate 7.3g Protein 27.8g

CHILE CON CARNE

A hint of chile and spices, fabulous with Guacamole (see page 202) and a tomato salad. Or you could scoop this up with small, crisp lettuce leaves, with the usual accompaniments like pickled jalapeños and sour cream.

Serves 6

1 onion, peeled and cut into pieces
2 slim carrots, trimmed, peeled, and chopped
1 rib of celery, chopped
2 tablespoons unsalted butter
1 tablespoon extra virgin olive oil
1 tablespoon finely chopped or sliced medium-hot red chile
2 tablespoons fresh oregano or marjoram leaves, or 1 teaspoon dried
4 garlic cloves, peeled and finely chopped
1 heaping teaspoon ground cumin
1¾ lbs lean ground beef
⅔ cup red wine
1 × 14oz can chopped tomatoes
1 tablespoon tomato paste
⅔ cup chicken or beef stock
sea salt
a couple of handfuls of coarsely chopped fresh cilantro, plus extra to serve

Put the onion, carrot, and celery in the bowl of a food processor and process until finely chopped. Heat the butter and the olive oil in a medium saucepan over medium heat, and cook the vegetable mixture with the chile and fresh oregano or marjoram for about 10 minutes until softened and glossy, stirring frequently and adding the garlic and cumin just before the end.

Add the ground beef, turn up the heat, and cook, stirring frequently, until the meat changes color. Add the wine, tomatoes, paste, stock, and oregano if using dried, and season with salt. Bring to a boil, then simmer over low heat for 1 hour, stirring now and again. The juices should be rich and well reduced. Skim off any excess fat, stir in the cilantro, and taste for seasoning. Serve with extra cilantro sprinkled on top.

Carbohydrate 6.3g Protein 31.2g

HERBY LAMB RAGÙ

I love the liveliness of this ragù with its spices, herbs, and orange juice, leaning toward the east of the Mediterranean.

Serves 6

3 tablespoons extra virgin olive oil
4 shallots, peeled and finely
    chopped
3 garlic cloves, peeled and finely
    chopped
⅓ teaspoon ground allspice
⅓ teaspoon ground cinnamon
2 lbs lean ground lamb
1⅔ cups smooth orange juice
2 heaping tablespoons tomato paste
sea salt
cayenne pepper
2 bunches of scallions (8–10
    in each), trimmed and sliced
1 handful of coarsely chopped
    cilantro
1 handful of coarsely chopped
    flat-leaf parsley

Heat 2 tablespoons of olive oil in a medium-large saucepan over medium heat and cook the shallots for a minute or so until softened and translucent, stirring frequently, then stir in the garlic and spices and cook for another minute. Add the lamb, turn up the heat, and cook until the meat changes color. Add the orange juice, the tomato paste, some salt, and a little cayenne pepper, bring to a boil, then cover and cook over low heat for 1 hour.

Leave the ragù to stand for 5 minutes. Heat a large frying pan over high heat, toss the scallions with the remaining tablespoon of oil and cook for several minutes until softened and golden, stirring frequently—they will reduce considerably during the cooking. Skim any excess fat off the ragù juices, stir in the herbs, transfer the ragù to a warm gratin or shallow serving dish, and sprinkle with the scallions.

Carbohydrate 8.7g Protein 35.4g

Jerk chicken

You can buy Caribbean jerk mix, deliciously heady with allspice, thyme, cayenne, nutmeg and cloves. Blend it with lemon, garlic, and olive oil, and you have an instant marinade. Chicken tenders, which are basically the small fillet that runs below the main fillet, are great here since they cook through in minutes, and because they are slim they turn nicely feisty by absorbing lots of the marinade. Guacamole is good here (see page 202), and a tomato salad. As are little pitas or tacos if you're catering for teenagers, too.

Serves 6

Marinade:
2 tablespoons lemon juice
3 tablespoons extra virgin olive oil
1 garlic clove, peeled and crushed
   to a paste
2 teaspoons jerk seasoning

Chicken:
1¾ lbs free-range chicken tenders
sea salt

Up to a couple of hours in advance of eating, combine all the marinade ingredients in a bowl or airtight plastic container. Carefully slice either side of the chicken's white tendon if it is present, and remove it. Add the chicken to the marinade and coat it. Cover and chill if not cooking right away.

Heat a large, nonstick frying pan over medium heat, season the chicken tenders with salt, and cook in batches for a couple of minutes on each side, until golden and firm when pressed.
Carbohydrate 0.7g Protein 32.1g

Marinated chicken thighs

I'm a huge fan of chicken thighs, which combine everything that's good about the breast with the succulence and added flavor of the dark meat. They're streets ahead of drumsticks, but when they cook bone-in they also have the same advantages. So these make great snacking.

Serves 4

Marinade:
juice of 1 lemon
4 tablespoons extra virgin olive oil
3 garlic cloves, peeled and crushed
    to a paste
1 teaspoon paprika

Chicken:
8 free-range chicken thighs
sea salt and freshly ground black
    pepper

Whisk all the marinade ingredients together in a large bowl or airtight plastic container. Add the chicken thighs, and coat thoroughly with the marinade. Cover and leave in the fridge for a couple of hours or overnight, turning them once.

Preheat the oven to 425°F and line the base of a shallow roasting pan with foil. Season the thighs on both sides and lay them on a rack inside the pan. Spoon on a little of the marinade and cook for 30–35 minutes until the outside is golden and the flesh comes away from the bone with ease. These can be eaten hot or cold.
Carbohydrate 0.7g Protein 40.5g

BARBECUED
Season the chicken thighs on both sides and barbecue for 30–50 minutes in total, turning them as necessary, and starting them off well away from the coals to ensure they cook through without burning.

Sausage and onion roast

The majority of French sausages, or *saucisses*, are made with 100 percent meat, give or take the spices, onion and other flavorings, but certainly with no rusk or bread fillers. Increasingly, U.S. producers are starting to follow suit, given the demand for gluten-free sausages and also ones without any carbs, so it is now possible to buy a good selection in most supermarkets. A bowl of buttery veg mash is as welcome as ever, such as the Spring root mash (see page 162).

Serves 6

5 tablespoons extra virgin olive oil
2⅔ lbs pork sausages
6 red onions, peeled, halved, and
    sliced
6 leeks, trimmed and thickly sliced
a small bunch of thyme (about
    15 sprigs)
sea salt and freshly ground black
    pepper

Heat a tablespoon of oil in a large frying pan over medium heat and brown the sausages on both sides, in two batches if you need to, then transfer them to a large bowl. Arrange the onions, leeks, and thyme sprigs on the base of one or two roasting pans (I use a 10 × 15 inch pan, and a smaller 8 × 12 inch pan)—the vegetables need to be about an inch deep. Drizzle with the remaining oil and season, then arrange the sausages on top, spaced about 2 inches apart.

Preheat the oven to 375°F and bake the sausages and vegetables for 1 hour, stirring every 20 minutes until the vegetables are silky and colored; they will reduce considerably in the process of cooking. Discard the thyme sprigs as you serve the sausages with the vegetables.
Carbohydrate 13.2g Protein 51g

WITH MUSTARD SAUCE
For a creamy mustard sauce to go with the sausages, while they are roasting, blend 1 cup **sour cream** with 1½ tablespoons **Dijon mustard** in a bowl (this can be done well in advance). You could also sprinkle in some coarsely chopped **flat-leaf parsley**.
Carbohydrate 15g Protein 52.4g

Eggplant-wrapped Greek sausages with roast tomatoes

Bend your imagination to a heart of sausage encased in a succulent eggplant wrap. For a full Greek spread, you could serve this with toasted halloumi cheese and a big salad of Romaine leaves, and some Tzatziki, too (see page 81).

Serves 4

1⅓ lbs lean ground lamb
1 shallot, peeled and finely chopped
1 garlic clove, peeled and crushed
    to a paste
1 teaspoon ground cumin
¼ teaspoon red pepper flakes
sea salt and freshly ground black
    pepper
2 good-sized eggplants, ends
    removed
extra virgin olive oil
1 lb mixed red and yellow cherry
    and grape tomatoes, halved
4 tablespoons fresh oregano leaves

To make the sausages, blend the ground lamb, shallot, garlic, cumin, red pepper flakes, and a little salt in a bowl. Taking a heaping tablespoon of the mixture at a time, form into 12 spindle-shaped sausages around 3 inches long. Heat a large, nonstick frying pan over high heat and brown these all over, then set aside. You will probably need to do this in two batches.

Preheat the oven to 425°F. Slice off the outer edge of each eggplant lengthwise and reserve these outer slices for another use. Then thinly slice each eggplant lengthwise to give you 6 slices (12 in all). Heat a clean large, nonstick frying pan over high heat, brush as many eggplant slices as will fit in a single layer with oil on one side, and season. Cook oiled-side down for 1½–2 minutes, then brush the top side with oil and cook likewise. They don't need to be fully cooked through, just colored. Remove to a plate and cook the remainder in the same fashion.

Starting at the rounded end of each eggplant slice, roll up a sausage, skewer with a toothpick and arrange in a large roasting pan (about 10 × 15 inches) with a little space between each. Toss the tomatoes with half of the oregano, some seasoning, and a couple of tablespoons of oil and scatter over and among the rolls. Sprinkle on the remaining oregano, drizzle with a little more oil, and bake for 30–35 minutes until everything is nice and golden.
Carbohydrate 8.9g Protein 31.7g

A skewer or two

Here are a couple of very easy skewers that are particularly good for a barbecue, both of which are delicious served with Tzatziki (see page 81), or the AKA potato salad (see page 202). For a hand-held skewer, slip the lamb or chicken pieces off the skewer onto a large Romaine leaf and slather with the Tzatziki. Some Crispy roast onions (see page 166) are also very welcome.

LOULOU SKEWERS
These are like spicy hamburgers on sticks, and a great favorite in our house.

Makes 8

1½ lbs lean ground lamb
1 shallot, peeled and finely chopped
2 tablespoons finely chopped
    flat-leaf parsley
½ teaspoon each ground cumin,
    cinnamon, and nutmeg
sea salt and freshly ground black
    pepper

Combine all the ingredients for the skewers with 1½ teaspoons of salt and some black pepper using your hands, then divide the mixture into 8 balls the size of a small apple. Shape each one of these into a long, flat sausage 4–5 inches in length and about an inch wide and slip a skewer lengthwise through the middle so the tip is just concealed by the end of the skewer. Set these aside on a plate—they can be made up to 24 hours in advance, in which case cover and chill them.

Place a ridged cast-iron grill pan over medium-high heat and grill the skewers for about 15 minutes in all, cooking them on all 4 sides. You may need to cook them in batches. Accompany with Tzatziki (see page 81).
Carbohydrate 0.5g Protein 16.4g

BARBECUE
Barbecue the skewers for 15–20 minutes in total, turning them as necessary and cooking them on all 4 sides.

PAPRIKA CHICKEN SKEWERS

While pieces of vegetable between morsels of chicken on a skewer always look colorful, they never grill very well. I prefer a skewer crammed with chicken cheek to cheek, roasting some onions separately to combine with the meat at the end (see page 166).

Makes 6

Marinade:
juice of 1 lemon
4 tablespoons extra virgin olive oil
3 garlic cloves, peeled and crushed
    to a paste
2 teaspoons paprika
1 tablespoon fresh thyme leaves

Chicken:
6 skinless free-range chicken
    breasts
sea salt and freshly ground black
    pepper

Whisk together all the ingredients for the marinade in a large bowl or airtight plastic container. Remove the white tendon beneath each chicken breast, then cut them into hearty cubes, about 2 inches, add to the bowl, and coat thoroughly with the marinade. Cover and leave in the fridge for a couple of hours or overnight. Season the chicken and thread onto 8-inch skewers (see tip below).

Place a ridged cast-iron grill pan (ideally a double one) over medium heat and grill the skewers on all 4 sides for 15–20 minutes in total. You may need to cook them in batches.
Carbohydrate 1.1g Protein 35.2g

BARBECUE
Season the chicken skewers and barbecue for 20–25 minutes in total, turning them as necessary, and starting them off well away from the coals to ensure they cook through without burning.

TZATZIKI

This makes a sizeable quantity, but my children adore it and we seem to get through it by the bucketload. It's great with both the chicken and the Loulou skewers on page 79.

Serves 6

2½ cups fat-free Greek yogurt
extra virgin olive oil
2 teaspoons lemon juice
1 garlic clove, peeled and crushed
    to a paste
4 tablespoons finely sliced mint
a pinch of sugar
sea salt and freshly ground black
    pepper
2 cucumbers

Blend the yogurt with 2 tablespoons of olive oil, the lemon juice, garlic, mint, sugar, and a little seasoning in a bowl. Peel the cucumbers, slit them in half lengthwise, and scoop out the seeds using a teaspoon. Now thinly slice them into half moons and stir these into the yogurt mixture. Check the seasoning, then pile it into a clean bowl and pour on a little olive oil. This can be made up to a couple of hours in advance, in which case cover and set aside somewhere cool.
Carbohydrate 5.1g Protein 9.1g

TIP: Bamboo skewers are prettier than metal ones, which can look a little fierce on the plate. They can be found in many supermarkets and come in different lengths. To prevent them from scorching, soak them in water before assembling the skewers.

*If you are using **metal skewers**, you will find that flat rather than round ones prevent the meat from slipping when you turn them.*

Spicy ribs

Barbecue marinades tend to be loaded with sugar or honey, which aids their caramelization. But I find you get equally golden ribs with this marinade, and the vinegar brings out the flavor of the pork. While ribs tend to be a fatty cut, it is this layering that allows them to slow-roast to such tender succulent results, and most of it renders in the throes of cooking and is drained off in any case. My preference is for St. Louis ribs. These are cut from the belly and are much meatier than baby back ribs; you may also encounter belly ribs, which are the same but without the rind. A crisp green salad and, as ever, it's fingers in.

Serves 6

Marinade:
4 tablespoons ketchup
4 tablespoons peanut oil
1 tablespoon mustard
2 tablespoons Worcestershire sauce
2 tablespoons dry sherry or
    Madeira
1 tablespoon red wine vinegar
4 garlic cloves, peeled and crushed
    to a paste
2 teaspoons finely grated fresh ginger
1 heaping teaspoon garam masala

Ribs:
4½ lbs free-range St. Louis ribs
sea salt
a handful of medium-hot red
    chiles (optional)

Whisk together all the ingredients for the marinade in a large bowl. Add the ribs, turning to coat them in the mixture. Cover and chill for at least 1 hour, ideally several. You can also marinate them overnight.

Preheat the oven to 350°F. Turn the ribs to coat them in the marinade and arrange in two roasting pans in a single layer spaced slightly apart, seasoning them on both sides with salt. Tuck in the chiles if using. Cover with foil and roast for 1 hour. Uncover the ribs and coat with any residual marinade—there should be some juices in the base of the pan—and roast for another 45 minutes or until golden and the juices have reduced to a sticky residue. Serve 15–20 minutes out of the oven once they are cool enough to handle, with chiles for those who wish to brave them.
Carbohydrate 4.4g Protein 31.9g

PIES & CASSEROLES

Pies are conceivably one of the trickiest of our favorite dishes to find a way around. Ultimately they are a casserole or stew, encased in carbs by the way of potatoes or pastry. But this can just as readily be a vegetable layer on top, and if the match is right this is no trading down. When it contributes to the ensemble and is in keeping with the filling—some crispy onions with beef, celeriac with lamb, zucchini with salmon, the vegetables will double up as a side dish. Which is not to stop you dishing up a big bowl of vegetable mash.

Casseroles, too, are all the better for being kept in the comfort zone. It is the juices or copious gravy that demands something to mop it up, and even though that might traditionally take the form of rice, pasta, potatoes, or polenta, a vegetable purée can be equally alluring, and you have the added advantage of being able to marry it to suit.

Cottage pie with leek and cauliflower mash

This delicate, pale green mash has that wholesome silky texture that is exclusive to leek soups and purées. Smothered with cherry tomatoes and scallions before being baked, the pie is every bit as lavish as the original. Don't worry too much about the ratio of leeks to cauliflower—you want more or less 2½ pounds in total but it doesn't matter too much how you get there.

Serves 6

Beef:
3 tablespoons unsalted butter
3 tablespoons extra virgin olive oil
2 slim carrots, trimmed, peeled, and thinly sliced
2 ribs celery heart, trimmed and thinly sliced
1 onion, peeled and finely chopped
2 tablespoons fresh oregano or marjoram leaves, or 1 tablespoon fresh thyme leaves
2¼ lbs lean ground beef
¾ cup red wine
1 × 14oz can chopped tomatoes
2 tablespoons tomato paste
2 teaspoons Worcestershire sauce
sea salt and freshly ground black pepper

Mash:
6 cups leeks, thickly sliced
6 cups small cauliflower florets
freshly grated nutmeg
a bunch of slim scallions, sliced
5oz small cherry tomatoes, halved

Heat half the butter and a tablespoon of olive oil in a medium saucepan over medium heat, add the sliced and chopped vegetables and herbs, and cook for 5–8 minutes, stirring occasionally, until softened and lightly colored. Add the meat, turn up the heat and cook, stirring occasionally, until it changes color. Add the red wine, chopped tomatoes and paste, Worcestershire sauce, and some seasoning. Bring to a simmer then cook over very low heat for 50–60 minutes, stirring occasionally, until nearly all the juices have been absorbed. Keep a careful eye on it toward the end to prevent it from burning. Tilt the pan and skim off any surface fat, then taste for seasoning.

While the meat cooks, start making the mash. Place the leeks and cauliflower in a large saucepan with ⅔ cup water, dot with the remaining butter, and add a tablespoon of olive oil and some salt. Bring the liquid to a simmer, then cover and cook over low heat for 15–25 minutes, stirring halfway through, until very tender. Transfer the contents of the pan into a food processor and reduce to a purée, seasoning it with nutmeg and more salt if necessary. You tend to get the best results if you do this in a couple of batches.

Transfer the meat to a shallow ovenproof dish or roasting pan (about 8 × 12 inches), pressing down to level the surface. Spread the mash on top. You can make the pie in advance, in which case leave to cool, cover and chill.

Preheat the oven to 400°F. Toss the scallions and cherry tomatoes with the remaining tablespoon of oil and spread over the surface. Bake for 40–45 minutes until the vegetables on top are golden.
Carbohydrate 13.3g Protein 43.8g

Celeriac cottage pie

Another cottage pie, but here the usual mashed potato is replaced with a celeriac purée. This vegetable has a particular affinity with beef, somehow they seek to outdo each other's bass notes. This pie is altogether more rugged than the preceding one, which only emphasizes how different vegetables can shape the character of a dish in a way that starchy carbs can't.

Serves 6

Meat:
1 carrot, trimmed, peeled and cut up
1 celery rib, cut up
1 onion, peeled and cut up
2 tablespoons extra virgin olive oil
2 teaspoons fresh thyme leaves
2 lbs lean ground beef
1¼ cups red wine
2 tablespoons tomato paste
⅔ cup beef or chicken stock
sea salt and freshly ground black
    pepper

Mash:
a splash of vinegar, (white wine or
    cider)
3⅓ lbs celeriac, skin cut off, and
    cut into chunks
7 tablespoons unsalted butter
freshly grated nutmeg
milk
2 large egg yolks

Finely chop the carrot, celery, and onion in a food processor. Heat the oil in a medium saucepan over medium heat, add the chopped vegetables and thyme, and cook for about 5 minutes, stirring occasionally, until softened. Add the ground beef, turn up the heat to high, and continue to cook, stirring frequently, until it changes color. Add the wine and simmer until well reduced, then stir in the tomato paste, the stock, and some seasoning, bring to a boil, and simmer over low heat for 30 minutes. Spoon off any excess fat from the surface.

While the meat is cooking, bring a large saucepan of water to a boil and acidulate it with a splash of vinegar. Add the celeriac and simmer for 20–30 minutes until tender, then drain in a colander, and leave for a few minutes for the surface moisture to evaporate.

Place the celeriac with the butter and some salt, pepper, and nutmeg in a blender, and purée, adding a drop of milk to kickstart the process. You'll probably need to do this in batches, transferring it to a bowl as you go. Stir in the egg yolks.

Transfer the meat to a shallow ovenproof dish or roasting pan (about 8 × 12 inches), pressing down to level the surface. Spread the celeriac on top. You can make the pie in advance, in which case leave to cool, then cover and chill.

Preheat the oven to 400°F and bake for 35–40 minutes.
Carbohydrate 10g Protein 38.5g

Autumn veggie lasagna

The creation of this lasagna was inspired by the French tradition of stuffed cabbage, which is one of the Gallic definitions of comfort, and truly delicious when carefully prepared, but a step too much for me. So this sets out to steal the spirit for an Italian great, by layering a richly flavored ragù with tender kale and sautéed mushrooms. A Celeriac or Cauliflower mash would both be lovely here (see pages 157 and 158).

Serves 6

Ragù:
4 tablespoons extra virgin olive oil
1 large onion, peeled and finely chopped
1 large carrot, peeled, halved lengthwise, and finely sliced
2 sticks celery, trimmed and finely sliced
3oz diced unsmoked bacon
2 garlic cloves, peeled and finely chopped
2¼ lbs lean ground beef
1¼ cups red wine
1 × 14oz can chopped tomatoes
¾ cup chicken stock
3 tablespoons tomato paste
1 bay leaf
sea salt and freshly ground black pepper

Vegetables:
7oz baby kale (trimmed weight)
14oz crimini mushrooms, stalks trimmed and sliced

Top:
2 heaping tablespoons crème fraîche
½ cup freshly grated Parmesan

To make the ragù, heat 2 tablespoons of olive oil in a large saucepan over medium heat, add the onion, carrot, celery, and bacon, and cook for 8–10 minutes until aromatic and lightly colored, stirring in the garlic just before the end. Add the beef and cook, stirring frequently, until it seals in the flavor and changes color. Pour in the red wine and simmer until this is well-reduced. Add the canned tomatoes, chicken stock, tomato paste, bay leaf, and a grinding of black pepper. Bring to a simmer, then cook over low heat for 40–45 minutes until almost all the liquid has evaporated, keeping an eye on it, and stirring toward the end. Leave the sauce to stand for a few minutes, then skim off any oil on the surface. Taste for salt—depending on the saltiness of the bacon, it may or may not require any extra. Discard the bay leaf.

While the ragù is simmering, bring a large saucepan of salted water to a boil, add the kale, and blanch for 2 minutes, then drain in a colander. To cook the mushrooms, heat a tablespoon of oil in a large frying pan over medium heat, add half the mushrooms, season, and cook for about 5 minutes, stirring frequently, until softened and golden and any liquid given out has evaporated. Transfer these to a bowl and cook the remainder in the same way.

Select a 8 × 12 inch roasting pan or baking dish of an equivalent size, and layer the ingredients as follows. Cover the base of the dish with a third of the ragù, then cover with half the greens then half the mushrooms, and repeat with the remaining ingredients, so that you end up with three layers of ragù and two of vegetables. If making the lasagna in advance, leave it to cool before dotting the crème fraîche over the top, and scattering with the Parmesan.

Preheat the oven to 400°F and bake the lasagna for 45 minutes or until golden and bubbling on the surface.
Carbohydrate 10.3g Protein 46.8g

Lamb casserole

Traditionally this is made using neck chops, but diced shoulder is always an option. Celeriac takes the place of the usual slices of potato, turning deliciously tender underneath and crispy on top.

Serves 6

1 tablespoon vegetable oil

3 tablespoons unsalted butter

sea salt and freshly ground black pepper

2⅔ lbs lamb shoulder, cut into 2-inch chunks

2 onions, peeled, halved, and thinly sliced

1¾ lbs carrots, trimmed, peeled, and cut diagonally into roughly 2-inch lengths

1 bay leaf

2 teaspoons Worcestershire sauce

1½ lbs celeriac (peeled weight)

Preheat the oven to 375°F. Heat the oil and half the butter in a large cast-iron casserole over medium heat, season the meat, and brown on all sides, working in batches so as not to overcrowd the casserole, removing it to a bowl as you go. Pour off the excess fat, leaving just a couple of tablespoons in the casserole. Add the onions and cook for several minutes until golden—keep a careful eye on the pan because this will happen quite quickly. Return the meat to the pan, add the carrots and the bay leaf, and stir to mix everything together. Stir the Worcestershire sauce into 3 cups of water and pour this in, and add some seasoning.

Cut the celeriac downward into four or eight wedges depending on its size, and thinly slice across—you can do this with the slicing attachment on a food processor. Level the lamb and carrots as far as possible (the liquid won't quite cover them), and bring to a boil. Layer the celeriac on top, seasoning the layers as you go, and dot with the remaining butter. Cover and cook in the oven for 1¼ hours, then uncover and cook for another hour until the celeriac is golden and crisp. You can also pop the casserole briefly under a hot broiler if you want to brown the top even more.

Carbohydrate 16.9g Protein 39.6g

Cheat's meatball moussaka

The cheat here is because the eggplant is roasted rather than grilled or fried, which also reduces the amount of fat it absorbs, the ragù is store-bought, and there is a speedy white sauce, which together make this one a cinch compared to the usual long-haul. I like to eat it scooped onto the small crisp leaves of a Romaine heart; the process of getting in there with my fingers takes me closer to a Greek taverna than a knife and fork.

Serves 6

Eggplants:
2 eggplants, ends discarded,
    cut into ½-inch slices
extra virgin olive oil
sea salt and freshly ground black
    pepper

Meatballs:
1¾ lbs lean ground lamb
1 heaping teaspoon dried oregano
½ teaspoon ground cinnamon
¼ teaspoon cayenne pepper
2 × 12oz jars tomato ragù,
    preferably Bertolli or Sacla

Sauce:
2½ cups fat-free Greek yogurt
2 large eggs, beaten
7oz "light" halloumi, grated
2 heaping tablespoons fresh
    oregano, or marjoram leaves, or
    1 heaping tablespoon lemon
    thyme leaves

Preheat the oven to 375°F. Lay the eggplant slices out on a baking sheet, brush both sides with oil, and season the top. Roast for 15 minutes, then turn the slices and cook for a further 10–15 minutes until golden.

In the meantime, mix together all the meatball ingredients except the ragù in a large bowl, seasoning the mixture with salt, then use your hands to roll it into balls the size of a walnut. Heat a large, nonstick frying pan over medium-high heat and brown the meatballs, half at a time, on all sides, draining off any fat between batches, then transfer them to a bowl. Carefully mix in the ragù.

Arrange the meatballs in a 12-inch oval gratin dish or one of similar size, and lay the eggplant slices on top, overlapping as necessary. Whisk the yogurt with the eggs in a medium bowl, then stir in half the halloumi. Spread on top of the eggplant layer and sprinkle on the remaining cheese. Toss the herbs with a tablespoon of oil and sprinkle over the surface. Bake for 40–45 minutes until puffy and golden. Serve 10–20 minutes out of the oven or, on a nice day, it is also delicious eaten warm rather than hot, in the Greek spirit.
Carbohydrate 14.8g Protein 46.8g

Imam bayildi

These eggplants, with their tomato and herb filling, will make a great meal for any vegetarians. So succulent, I'll go with the Imam fainting with pleasure on eating it rather than being shocked by the amount of oil, as the two contrasting legends about this dish go. I cannot imagine Turkish cooks divulged that kind of information to their great leaders; I imagine they played their cards very close in order to remain indispensable.

Serves 4

2 eggplants, stem end trimmed
extra virgin olive oil
sea salt and freshly ground black
    pepper
2 beefsteak tomatoes (about
    9oz each)
1 large onion, peeled, halved, and
    thinly sliced
5 garlic cloves, peeled, and finely
    chopped
3 tablespoons each coarsely
    chopped fresh flat-leaf parsley,
    dill, and basil

Preheat the oven to 400°F and heat a ridged cast-iron grill pan over medium heat for several minutes. Halve the eggplants lengthwise and brush them all over with oil. Season and grill the cut surface for about 5 minutes until golden, then lay the eggplant halves, cut-side up, in a roasting pan. You will probably need to grill them half at a time, depending on the size of your grill pan.

In the meantime bring a small saucepan of water to a boil and cut out the core from each tomato. Plunge them into a boiling water for about 20 seconds and then into cold water. Slip off their skins and coarsely chop them. Combine in a bowl with the onion, garlic, and herbs, add some seasoning and 6 tablespoons of olive oil, and toss.

Pile the vegetable mixture on top of the eggplants and roast for 40–45 minutes until the vegetables are nicely golden. Leave to cool for at least 15 minutes, and either serve warm or at room temperature with more olive oil poured on if wished.
Carbohydrate 13g Protein 3.7g

WITH OLIVES
Scatter some pitted **black olives** over the eggplants before serving them.
Carbohydrate 13g Protein 3.9g

Chicken and spinach pie with pumpkin mash

Many of the richest pies rely on a béchamel or white sauce, delicious but also off-limits when you start to consider what goes into it. So, a replacement? It has to be white, thick, and silky. I adore sauces that come with the word *soubise* attached, meaning based on onions, so this was the answer.

Serves 6

Chicken:
3 tablespoons extra virgin olive oil
sea salt and freshly ground black pepper
about 3½ lbs free-range chicken thighs and drumsticks
⅔ cup white wine
1 cup chicken stock or water
5 tablespoons unsalted butter, plus a pat
5 large onions, peeled, halved, and sliced
1 lb spinach, washed

Mash:
2⅔ lbs pumpkin flesh, cut into even-sized chunks
freshly grated nutmeg
3 tablespoons coarsely chopped flat-leaf parsley

Heat a tablespoon of olive oil in a large cast-iron casserole over medium-high heat. Season the chicken pieces and color on both sides, half at a time. Drain off the fat, return all the chicken to the pan, add the wine, and simmer to reduce by half. Pour in the chicken stock or water. Bring to a simmer, cover, and cook over low heat for 30 minutes, stirring halfway through.

In the meantime, melt 3 tablespoons of the butter in a large saucepan over low heat. Add the onions, sprinkle with a teaspoon of salt, and gently cook them for 30 minutes, stirring frequently to prevent them from coloring. By the end they should be lusciously silky and soft. While they cook, place the spinach in a large saucepan with just the water that clings to the leaves, cover, and cook over low heat for about 10 minutes, stirring halfway through, until it wilts. Drain into a sieve, pressing out the excess liquid with the back of a spoon, and coarsely chop.

Transfer the chicken pieces to a bowl and leave the juices to settle—the fat will rise to the top. Once cool enough to handle, remove and discard the skin and bones and coarsely shred the flesh. Skim the fat off the surface of the cooking juices, and place ⅔ cup of the juices in a blender with the onions and purée. Combine the shredded chicken and the sauce in a large bowl, and stir in the spinach. Transfer to a roasting pan or ovenproof dish (about 8 × 12 inches).

For the mash, either steam the pumpkin for 15–20 minutes until tender, or place it in a large saucepan with a couple of inches of water, bring to a boil, cover, and cook for a similar time. Drain in a sieve and press out the excess liquid using a potato masher. Transfer it to a large bowl and coarsely mash using a fork. Dice and stir in the remaining butter, 2 tablespoons of olive oil, some seasoning, and nutmeg, then fold in the parsley. Smooth the mash over the chicken and spinach, forking the surface into rough peaks. You can make the pie in advance, in which case leave to cool, cover and chill.

Preheat the oven to 400°F and bake the pie for 45 minutes. Heat the broiler, dot the pie with the pat of butter, and pop underneath until golden at the tips. *Carbohydrate 16.5g Protein 28.3g*

Braised pork and apple with a mushroom crust

You can almost hear the rustle of fallen leaves underfoot, such is the sense of autumn this braise offers with its apples and mushrooms. It will prove warming throughout the winter months whenever the weather is cold and you are after something truly hearty.

Serves 6

extra virgin olive oil
sea salt and freshly ground black
    pepper
2 lbs pork tenderloin, sliced into
    medallions 1 inch thick
4oz unsmoked lardons, or diced
    bacon
1 onion, peeled, quartered, and
    thinly sliced
2 garlic cloves, peeled and finely
    sliced
⅔ cup Madeira or medium-dry
    sherry
1⅔ cups chicken stock
1 eating apple, peeled, quartered,
    cored, and diced
1 cooking apple, peeled, quartered,
    cored, and diced
14oz crimini mushrooms, stalks
    trimmed and thinly sliced
4oz button mushrooms, stalks
    trimmed and halved
a handful of fresh sage leaves
sour cream, to serve (optional)

Preheat the oven to 300°F. Heat a tablespoon of oil in a large cast-iron casserole over medium-high heat, lightly season the pork (the bacon will do a lot of the work), and brown on both sides, just a few at a time so as not to overcrowd the pan, then transfer them to a bowl. You may need to add a drop of oil between batches. Turn the heat down to medium-low, add another tablespoon of oil to the pan, and cook the lardons or bacon for about 5 minutes until lightly colored, then add the onion and cook for another 5 minutes, stirring frequently, until golden and syrupy, adding the garlic just before the end.

Add the Madeira or sherry and stir to dissolve all the sticky residue on the bottom of the pan, then return the pork to the pan, pour in the stock, bring to a boil, cover, and cook in the oven for 2 hours.

Turn up the oven temperature to 400°F. Skim off any fat from the surface of the cooking juices, and stir the apples into the casserole. Toss the mushrooms with 2 tablespoons of oil in a large bowl, season and spread over the top. Sprinkle with the sage leaves and drizzle with another couple of tablespoons of oil. Return to the oven, uncovered, for 40–45 minutes until the sage leaves are crisp and the mushrooms turn a light gold. Tilt the casserole to skim off any fat from the surface of the juices, and serve with a spoonful of sour cream if wished.
Carbohydrate 9.6g Protein 36.5g

Red wine steak casserole with crispy onions

This is everything you dream of in a steak supper in casserole form. The beef is very slowly braised with red wine, juniper, and bacon, until meltingly tender and sitting in a rich, dark gravy, then finished in a hot oven with a layer of red onions that turn silky soft with a crispy top. A Broccoli mash would be lovely here (see page 158), or Carrot and rutabaga (see page 156).

Serves 6

Beef:

2 tablespoons unsalted butter

4oz unsmoked lardons, or diced bacon

sea salt and freshly ground black pepper

2⅔ lb braising beef (eg chuck or blade), cut into 1½ inch pieces

1 bay leaf

a few sprigs of fresh thyme

about 10 juniper berries, secured in a small square of cheesecloth

2½ cups red wine

⅔ cup beef stock

10oz small turnips, trimmed, peeled, and halved (or quartered if larger than a walnut)

Top:

1½ lbs red onions, peeled, halved, and thinly sliced

3 tablespoons vegetable oil

Preheat the oven to 300°F. Melt the butter in a large cast-iron casserole over medium heat and cook the lardons or bacon for about 5 minutes, stirring frequently until golden, then transfer to a bowl. Lightly season the beef and brown on all sides, in batches, in the residual fat, transferring to the bowl with the lardons or bacon when ready. If a lot of fat remains, pour this off before proceeding.

Return all the meat to the pan, add the herbs, juniper berries, wine, and stock, and season with black pepper (the bacon will provide some salt so this is best adjusted at the end of cooking). Bring to a simmer, skim off any foam on the surface, then cover and cook in the oven for 2½ hours, giving it a stir halfway through. Discard the herbs and spice bag. You can make the casserole in advance to this point, in which case leave to cool, cover and chill.

Turn up the oven temperature to 400°F. Skim off any fat from the surface of the sauce, and if necessary reheat on the stove. Stir the turnips into the casserole.

To make the topping, toss the onions with the oil in a large bowl, separating out the layers, and spread over the top. Return to the oven, uncovered, for another 55–60 minutes until the onions are golden and crisp on top.

Carbohydrate 12.2g Protein 46.3g

Ossobuco

For all the cachet attached to the name, this is a stew, and no more complex than any other we are accustomed to making. But it does have the added allure of a final sprinkle of gremolata, which whisks it out of its somnambulistic state after a couple of hours of slow cooking and back into the real world.

An authentic Ossobuco alla Milanese would not contain tomatoes (despite my own preference); if you are in any doubt about this, you should read Anna Del Conte's *Secrets from an Italian Kitchen*. Today they are frequently added, but for Anna this is a travesty. In place of a saffron risotto on the side, you could flavor the Cauliflower mash (see page 158) with saffron. Roast carrot wedges are lovely with it as well (see page 168).

The ideal here is thick slices of veal shank that will allow you to tie them to keep them in place, since thin slices are more likely to buckle when seared. If at all possible specify this to a butcher when buying. Either way, avoid small sections that will be all bone and no meat.

Serves 6

2⅔ lbs ossobuchi (ideally cut
    around 2 inches thick)
extra virgin olive oil
sea salt and freshly ground black
    pepper
1 tablespoon unsalted butter
1 onion, peeled, halved, and thinly
    sliced
2 carrots, trimmed, peeled, and
    sliced diagonally
1 celery heart, trimmed and sliced
    diagonally
2 garlic cloves, finely chopped
3 plum tomatoes, skinned and
    chopped
1 cup white wine
1¼ cups chicken stock
a pinch of red pepper flakes

Gremolata:
3 tablespoons finely chopped
    flat-leaf parsley
1 garlic clove, peeled and finely
    chopped
finely grated zest of 1 lemon

Preheat the oven to 325°F. Make a small nick in the skin surrounding the ossobuchi on either side—you will need a very sharp knife for this. If they are thick enough, then also tie a piece of string around each one. Heat a tablespoon of oil in a large frying pan over medium-high heat. Season the slices of veal and brown them on both sides, turning them frequently. You will need to do this in batches, replenishing the oil as necessary.

At the same time, heat 2 tablespoons of oil and the butter in a large cast-iron casserole over medium heat—choose one that will hold the pieces of veal as much as possible in a single layer. Add the onion, carrots, celery, and garlic and cook for 8–10 minutes, stirring frequently, until the vegetables are glossy and softened, without coloring. Stir in the tomatoes and cook for a minute longer, pressing them down. Nestle the ossobuchi among the vegetables. Pour in the wine and stock, and season with salt and a pinch of red pepper flakes. The tips of the meat may peek out at the top, but they should be more or less covered. Bring the liquid to a boil, then cover and cook in the oven for 2 hours. Check the meat halfway through and gently press down the pieces so they are evenly submerged. Avoid moving them around or the marrow may slip out from the center of the bone, and this is the great treat.

Combine the parsley, garlic and lemon zest for the gremolata and serve sprinkled over the meat.
Carbohydrate 7.2g Protein 27.5g

THICKENED JUICES
If you're not avoiding carbs, then you can also dip the pieces of meat into **flour** before cooking them, which will thicken the sauce just slightly.

Braised oxtail and onions

Many butchers will be able to provide you with oxtail, though it's worth a phone call a couple of days in advance to make sure they set some aside. You need good-sized pieces—the last few tapered sections of the tail are fine for stock but don't have any meat on them to speak of. Equally, you could use any other cut of braising steak here. In this case, you can reduce the cooking time to a couple of hours.

Serves 6

Marinade:
⅔ cup Madeira or medium sherry
2 garlic cloves, peeled and crushed
    to a paste
a few sprigs of fresh thyme
1 bay leaf, torn into pieces
¼ teaspoon ground cinnamon
¼ teaspoon ground nutmeg

Oxtail:
4½ lbs oxtail, separated into joints
extra virgin olive oil
sea salt and freshly ground black
    pepper
4 large onions, peeled, halved, and
    sliced
1 bottle red wine
10oz small chestnut or button
    mushrooms, stalks trimmed

To serve:
4 tablespoons chopped flat-leaf
    parsley mixed with finely grated
    zest of 1 orange

It isn't essential to marinate the meat, but it does give the dish that extra something. Combine the marinade ingredients in a large bowl, add the meat and baste it, cover and chill for about 6 hours or overnight, basting it halfway through if you remember.

Remove the meat from the marinade, and drain it on a double thickness of paper towels. Heat a tablespoon of olive oil in a large frying pan over highish heat, season, and add half the meat and brown it on all sides. Remove it and cook the remainder in the same way—there shouldn't be any need to add more oil.

Heat a couple of tablespoons of oil in a large cast-iron casserole over medium-high heat, add the onions, and cook for 10–15 minutes, stirring occasionally, until golden. Add the marinade, the wine, some seasoning, and then the oxtail. Bring to a boil, cover, and cook over low heat for 2 hours, giving it a stir halfway through.

Heat another couple of tablespoons of oil in a large frying pan over medium-high heat, add the mushrooms, season them, and sauté for a few minutes until lightly colored. Stir these into the casserole and simmer for another hour until the meat is fork tender.

Transfer the meat and mushrooms to a bowl, and simmer the juices to reduce them by about a third, discarding the herbs. Return the meat and mushrooms to the sauce and serve. The casserole can also be made in advance, in which case leave to cool and then chill, and remove any fat from the surface before reheating. Serve sprinkled with the chopped parsley and orange.
Carbohydrate 10.5g Protein 27.9g

Goulash

I like to cook chuck steak as a single large piece (as well as diced), which is more in keeping with the casserole cuts that I find in France, where the pieces are cut larger and cooked to the point at which the meat pulls apart with a fork, rendering lovely long, succulent strands. If you can't find it prepacked in the supermarket, it isn't insurmountable; ask your butcher.

Serves 6

Casserole:
extra virgin olive oil
sea salt and freshly ground black
    pepper
1 × 2⅔ lbs chuck steak in one
    piece
2 onions, peeled, halved, and thinly
    sliced
2 green peppers, cored, seeded,
    and cut into thin strips
2 red peppers, cored, seeded, and
    cut into thin strips
2 teaspoons sweet paprika (mild)
1 teaspoon caraway seeds
1 × 14oz can chopped tomatoes
1 cup red wine
1 cup beef stock

To serve:
sour cream
coarsely chopped flat-leaf parsley

Preheat the oven to 325°F. Heat a tablespoon of oil in a large cast-iron casserole over medium-high heat, season, and brown the meat on all sides. Remove and turn the heat down a little, add another couple of tablespoons of oil to the pan, and cook the onions for several minutes, stirring frequently, until starting to color, then add the peppers and cook for a few minutes longer.

Stir in the paprika and the caraway seeds, then add the tomatoes, wine, beef stock, and some salt and bring to a boil. Nestle the meat among the vegetables, cover, and cook in the oven for 3½ hours, turning the beef halfway through, by which time it should be meltingly tender. Taste for seasoning, and serve with a spoon of sour cream and lots of chopped parsley.
Carbohydrate 10.6g Protein 44.6g

Ultimate coq au vin

This classic casserole with its rich red wine gravy, button mushrooms and baby onions is one by which we judge many others. My treasured copy of Len Deighton's *Où est Le Garlic* seems to have gone missing, but I am quite sure that it must be in it. If you grew up at the end of the twentieth century without this dish being a fixture on the dinner table, you were deprived.

The ideal here is a whole chicken that has been cut into about eight pieces, but a mixture of thighs and drumsticks will also do nicely. Mash turns this into the ultimately comforting meal. The red wine doesn't need to be anything special: cheap, cheerful, and with plenty of character.

This is a casserole that reheats well, with the added advantage if you allow it to cool completely that you can remove any fat that has risen and set on the surface.

Serves 4

1 tablespoon vegetable oil
sea salt and freshly ground black
    pepper
3½ lbs free-range chicken, cut
    into 6–8 pieces, or a mixture of
    thighs and drumsticks
3oz diced unsmoked bacon or
    lardons
2½ cups red wine
⅔ cup chicken stock
1 bay leaf
2 sprigs of fresh thyme
1 tablespoon unsalted butter
7oz baby onions, or small shallots,
    peeled
4oz button mushrooms, stalks
    trimmed if necessary
coarsely chopped flat-leaf parsley
    to serve

Preheat the oven to 300°F. Heat the oil over medium-high heat in a large cast-iron casserole. Season the chicken pieces and brown on both sides, in batches. Transfer them to a bowl and pour off the fat, add the bacon or lardons, and cook until they just begin to color. Pour off all but a tablespoon of the fat. Return the chicken to the casserole. Pour in the red wine and chicken stock, and add the bay leaf and thyme. Heat the liquid until it just begins to bubble, then cover the casserole with a lid and cook in the oven for 1½ hours until the chicken is tender, turning the pieces on top halfway through. You can prepare the casserole to this point in advance, in which case leave to cool, cover and chill.

Either when you remove the casserole from the oven or just before serving it, melt the butter in a nonstick frying pan over low heat. Cook the onions for 15 minutes, turning them frequently, adding the mushrooms 5–7 minutes before the end. They should all be lightly golden. In the meantime, transfer the chicken pieces to a large bowl, carefully skim off any fat floating on the surface of the casserole, and reduce the sauce by half, continuing to skim off any fat that rises to the surface. Return the chicken to the sauce, cover and gently reheat if necessary. Add the onions and mushrooms, taste for seasoning and serve right away on warm plates, sprinkled with parsley.
Carbohydrate 2.6g Protein 56.1g

THICKENED JUICES
If you want to thicken the sauce slightly, after the chicken is returned to the casserole, sprinkle in 1 heaping tablespoon **flour** and cook, turning the pieces, for about 1 minute.
Carbohydrate 5.7g Protein 56.5g

Slow-roast pork shoulder with rosemary and anchovies

Slowly braised shoulder of pork is a great pot roast, and I often opt for this over a classic roast as it guarantees to be tender and succulent, and I adore that "pulled," falling-apart texture. Roasting pork can be hit and miss however carefully you approach the time and temperature.

But there is no need to do without the crackling. Ask your butcher to slice off the rind, so the fat is evenly distributed between meat and skin, and to score it and then to retie the roast for you. You can then roast the rind separately, turning up the oven temperature at the end to crisp it. Buttery spinach would be a good choice of vegetable with this, and as ever some kind of mash—broccoli springs to mind.

Serves 6

⅓ teaspoon red pepper flakes
4½ pounds boned, rolled shoulder of pork, rind removed and scored
sea salt
1 tablespoon extra virgin olive oil
½ bottle of white wine
1⅔ cups chicken stock
4 salted anchovies, sliced
3 garlic cloves, peeled and smashed
3 sprigs of fresh rosemary, about 2 inches long

Preheat the oven to 325°F. Rub the red pepper flakes over the pork (don't worry about the ends) and very lightly season with salt. Heat the oil in a large frying pan over medium-high heat and brown the pork all over, then transfer it to a large cast-iron casserole, placing it fat-side down. Add the wine, stock, anchovies, garlic, and rosemary, bring to a boil, then cover and cook in the oven for 5 hours. Turn the pork halfway through, and at the same time rub some salt into the pork rind, put it skin-side up in a small roasting pan, and then place in the oven.

Transfer the pork to a warm plate to rest for 20 minutes, loosely covering it with foil. In the meantime, turn up the oven temperature to 475°F to crisp the crackling for 10–15 minutes. You should see small bubbles appear below the surface.

Pour the juices into a pitcher, ideally transparent, and leave to rest for a minute or two for the oil to rise, then skim this off along with as much of the rosemary as possible. Return the juices to the pan and simmer to reduce by about a third until well flavored. The meat should be meltingly tender and pull apart with ease with a fork and spoon. Serve it with the juices and crackling.
Carbohydrate 2.8g Protein 62g

Guinea hen braised with saffron and black olives

We don't have to save saffron and black olives for summer—they bring just as much sunshine in the midst of winter. But try to find a good-sized guinea fowl, or buy two and freeze what you don't require for this recipe. If guinea hen isn't available, you can substitute chicken.

Serves 4

extra virgin olive oil
sea salt and freshly ground black pepper
1 × 3-lb guinea hen (or chicken), cut in serving pieces
8 shallots, peeled
1 celery heart, trimmed and cut into 2-inch lengths
⅔ cup dry vermouth
1 × 14oz can chopped tomatoes
½ cup chicken stock
about 25 saffron filaments, ground and blended with 1 tablespoon boiling water
a pinch of red pepper flakes
1 bay leaf
12 pitted green and black olives

Heat about a teaspoon of oil in a large frying pan over medium heat, season the guinea fowl (or chicken) pieces, and brown them on both sides, probably in batches. At the same time, heat a couple of tablespoons of oil in a large cast-iron casserole over medium heat, add the shallots and celery, and cook for 5–7 minutes, stirring occasionally, until glossy and lightly colored. Add the guinea fowl pieces, the vermouth, tomatoes, stock, saffron, red pepper flakes, bay leaf, and some salt. Give everything a good stir, arranging the guinea fowl pieces so as far as possible they are submerged. Bring the liquid to a boil, then cover and cook over low heat for 1 hour, adding the olives halfway through.

The casserole can be prepared a day in advance, in which case leave to cool, cover, and chill. To serve, skim off any fat on the surface, and reheat if necessary.
Carbohydrate 5.1g Protein 48.4g

Pot-roast rabbit with pastis

I tend to think of rabbit as a treat because we only rarely eat it in our house, most often when we are in France, where it is readily available, but it's starting to be more easily available elsewhere. Rabbit makes for a fine lunch if you have friends over, a touch more sophisticated than chicken, though not dissimilar. It revels in mustard and other lively flavors—here the French liqueur pastis and lemon. You could also serve the sautéed liver scattered over some vegetables on the side, such as a root vegetable mash, or some cabbage.

Serves 4

2 tablespoons Dijon mustard
1 rabbit, cut into 8 pieces,
    liver sliced and reserved
7 tablespoons unsalted butter,
    clarified*
2oz diced unsmoked bacon or
    lardons
1 lb baby leeks cut into 2-inch
    lengths, or regular leeks sliced
    ½-inch thick
1 bay leaf
2 sprigs of fresh thyme
⅔ cup pastis, preferably Ricard
juice of ½ lemon
½ cup chicken stock, or water
sea salt and freshly ground black
    pepper
chopped dill fronds, to serve

Preheat the oven to 300°F. Brush the mustard over the rabbit pieces. Heat a large cast-iron casserole over medium-high heat, add all but a tablespoon of the clarified butter, and brown the rabbit in batches, transferring the pieces to a plate as they are ready. Add the lardons to the pan and cook for a few minutes, stirring occasionally, until they begin to color.

Add the leeks to the pan with the herbs and continue to cook for about 7 minutes, stirring occasionally, until glossy and lightly colored. Return the rabbit to the pan, pour in the pastis, lemon juice, and stock or water. Lightly season (bearing in mind the bacon and mustard will do most of the work), then give everything a good stir, settling the rabbit pieces down as far as possible, though they won't be completely covered by the liquid. Cover and cook in the oven for 2 hours, turning the rabbit halfway through.

Transfer the cooked rabbit to a dish and simmer the juices vigorously for a few minutes to concentrate the flavors. Heat the reserved butter in a small frying pan over high heat, add the liver, and cook briefly until it changes color and seems just firm, then season it. Return the rabbit to the sauce, and serve sprinkled with the liver and a little dill.

Carbohydrate 13.3g Protein 30.9g

---

*TIP: **To clarify butter** gently melt it then skim off the surface foam, pour into a small jar, and reserve the clear butter and discard the milky residue below.*

THE CARVING BOARD

Protein is the key to success in avoiding carbs. No other food type sustains you in the same way—you feel nourished, full, but never overloaded or weighed down, and that satisfaction lasts for a long time. You don't get that rebound hunger as you do after a piece of fruit or a slice of toast or a muffin. In fact it's quite hard to eat too much, as you tend to stop when your body's had enough.

This chapter is a round-up of my stock favorite roasts, those that I turn to midweek, and without fail at the weekend. Even if there are only two of us, it provides the wherewithal for grazing thereafter. A roast itself is the most basic of dishes—it's all the accompaniments that constitute the hard work. Preparing a bird or a cut of meat for the oven usually takes around 5–10 minutes, so it's a good gain for minimal input. Another misconception is that roasts are very expensive, but, aside from a treat such as a leg of lamb or sirloin roast, most are considerably more affordable than prepared meals to feed the same number, or any other convenience food you are likely to buy.

Rustic garlic roast chicken

Chicken roasted with garlic is a fabulous dish, but peeling all those heads is too fiddly to bother with on an average weekday, or even weekend, and this rustic version, with the bird surrounded by whole heads, is just as good. With lemon, butter, and thyme, it is the perfect marriage of flavors.

The best accompaniment is a crisp green salad, and if you forego a dressing, you might just be able to justify drizzling the buttery juices from the roasting pan over the leaves.

Serves 4

a bunch of fresh lemon thyme
1 × 3½ lb free-range chicken,
untrussed
sea salt and freshly ground black
pepper
4 heads of garlic, tops cut off
3 tablespoons unsalted butter,
melted
1 lemon, halved

Preheat the oven to 400°F. Spread two-thirds of the thyme sprigs over the base of a roasting pan that will accommodate the chicken with a little room to spare around the sides, place the chicken on top, and season it. Pull half the thyme leaves off the remaining sprigs and sprinkle over the chicken with the sprigs, then surround with the garlic heads. Drizzle the butter over the chicken and the garlic, squeeze on the lemon juice, and pop the lemon halves inside the cavity of the bird. Roast for 50–55 minutes, basting the garlic halfway through.

Leave the chicken to rest in the pan for 15 minutes, then transfer both the chicken and the garlic to a warm plate, pouring any juices inside the bird back into the pan. Carve the chicken, adding any juices that have collected to the pan. Discard the thyme sprigs and rewarm the juices, skimming off the butter first if wished. Spoon the juices over the chicken, accompanied by the garlic, squeezing it out of its casing as you eat.
Carbohydrate 3.7g Protein 52.2g

Serves 6

… OR Guinea hen OR CORNISH HENS
For a slightly more special occasion or when you are feeding six people, then you could roast two **guinea hen** (about 2½ lbs each) or **Cornish hens** with six **heads of garlic**. Space them slightly apart in a roasting pan, place ½ **lemon** inside each bird, and increase the **butter** to 5 tablespoons and roast for 45–50 minutes then leave to rest as before.
Carbohydrate 5.8g Protein 58.5g

Lemon and spice roast chicken

This is one of my favorite methods for a simple weekday chicken. I endlessly play around with the spices. Quite often it's za'atar or another Middle Eastern blend, maybe a curry powder, and the thyme is optional. So treat it as a blueprint.

I think this one is a lovely summery roast, even more so if you serve it with the fattoush. The chicken emerges with a deep golden skin, and the pan juices take the place of gravy, which makes it all the more relaxing as it is one less task to complete before eating.

Serves 4

2 tablespoons extra virgin olive oil
2 tablespoons lemon juice
½ teaspoon paprika
¼ teaspoon allspice
1 tablespoon thyme leaves
1 × 3½ lb free-range chicken, untrussed
sea salt

Ideally marinate the chicken overnight, but it isn't the end of the world if you don't. Combine the oil with the lemon juice, the spices, and thyme in a bowl. Spoon this over the chicken in a roasting pan, coating the surface of the skin. If marinating the chicken overnight, cover the dish with plastic wrap and chill.

Preheat the oven to 400°F. Baste the chicken with any juices that have run down into the dish, season with salt and roast for 55 minutes, basting it a couple of times during roasting. Leave the chicken to rest in the pan for 20 minutes.

Transfer the chicken to a plate, pouring any juices inside the bird back into the pan, then skim off the excess fat. Carve the chicken and serve with the juices spooned over, accompanied by the salad if wished.
Carbohydrate 0.7g Protein 50.6g

Serves 4

1 cucumber, peeled, halved lengthways, and thickly sliced
7oz radishes, trimmed and quartered
10oz baby plum or cherry tomatoes, halved
1 small red onion, peeled, halved, and thinly sliced
a large handful each of mint leaves and flat-leaf parsley
3 tablespoons extra virgin olive oil
2 tablespoons lemon juice
sea salt

WITH FATTOUSH
This salad usually contains bread, but it is just as delightful without—the vegetables as an ensemble are crisp and clean, and you can add diced feta and olives to fill it out, too. This makes a large bowlful, which I find is not overdoing it for three or four, even though at a glance it easily serves six.

Place the cucumber, radishes, and tomatoes in a large bowl with the onion, separating out the layers. Tear the mint leaves in half and coarsely chop the parsley, and toss with the salad vegetables. You can prepare the salad to this point in advance, in which case cover the vegetables with plastic wrap and set aside somewhere cool.

Just before eating, pour the oil and lemon juice over the vegetables, season with salt, and toss.
Carbohydrate 4.7g Protein 51.9g

Roast chicken with a watercress crust

Don't be alarmed by the amount of butter involved in the roasting—it mainly serves to baste the bird as it cooks and is spooned off at the end. The watercress makes for a thick, succulent bank of stuffing beneath the skin, far more delicate than a bread-crumb stuffing inside the bird.

Serves 6

1 lemon
5 tablespoons unsalted butter, softened
sea salt and freshly ground black pepper
3–4oz watercress
2 tablespoons capers, rinsed and finely chopped
1 × 4½ lb free-range chicken, untrussed

Preheat the oven to 425°F. Zest the lemon and blend with 3 tablespoons of the butter and some seasoning in a large bowl. (If your butter is on the hard side, cream it in a food processor first.) Pulse the watercress in a clean food processor to finely chop it, and work into the butter with the capers. Using your hands, gently squeeze out the excess liquid.

Starting at the neck end of the chicken slip your fingers beneath the skin to loosen it over the breasts. Gently smooth half the watercress butter over each breast and pat the skin back into place, spreading the butter out evenly. Rub the remaining butter over the chicken. Place it in a roasting pan that accommodates it quite snugly, halve the lemon, and squeeze the juice over the bird, pop the halves inside the cavity, then season.

Roast for 1 hour then remove the chicken from the oven and transfer to a warm plate to rest for 15–20 minutes, pouring any juices inside the bird back into the pan. Skim any fat off the roasting juices, add about 6 tablespoons of water and simmer, taking up all the sticky residue from the base, then pass through a sieve. Carve the chicken, adding any juices that have collected to the gravy.
Carbohydrate 0.4g Protein 42.7g

Provençal pot roast with pistou

Pot roasts are great at providing the gravy or a sauce, as well as making for a particularly succulent bird as it is "wet-roasted." This one, with its Mediterranean flair of tomatoes, olives, and basil, has the edge over pot roasts that are laced with cream and thickened with flour.

Serves 4

2 beefsteak tomatoes
extra virgin olive oil
1 × 3½ lb free-range chicken, untrussed
sea salt and freshly ground black pepper
3 medium or 2 large onions, peeled, halved, and sliced
3 garlic cloves, peeled and finely sliced
2 sprigs of fresh rosemary
1 small dried red chile, finely chopped
⅔ cup white wine
4 large handfuls of basil leaves
2 cups pitted green and black olives

Bring a medium saucepan of water to a boil. Cut out the core of each tomato, plunge them into the water for about 20 seconds, and then into cold water. Slip off the skins and coarsely chop them.

Heat a large cast-iron casserole over a medium-high heat. Pour a little olive oil into the palm of your hand, rub your hands together, and coat the chicken all over. Season it with salt and pepper and place in the casserole to brown on all sides. Transfer it to a plate and turn the heat down. Add another couple of tablespoons of oil and cook the onions for about 5 minutes, stirring frequently, until softened and translucent—they may color a little. Once the heat calms down, you can turn it up a little. Add the garlic a minute or so before the end.

Add the tomatoes, the rosemary, chile, wine, and some salt, and settle the chicken into the sauce. Bring the liquid to a simmer, cover, and cook over low heat for 1 hour. While the chicken is cooking, place the basil leaves in a food processor with ½ cup of olive oil and a little salt and reduce to a purée.

Remove the chicken from the heat and transfer to a warm plate, pouring any juices inside the bird back into the pan, and leave to rest for 15 minutes. Leave the juices to stand for 5–10 minutes for the oil to rise, then skim it off and reduce the juices by half to concentrate the flavor. Carve the chicken and serve with the sauce spooned over, and a little of the pistou, scattered with olives.
Carbohydrate 14.9g Protein 52.5g

Rare roast beef with gravy

Thin slices of rare beef and a river of golden gravy is a kitchen essential. This less traditional method of roasting is my default. The lower temperature makes for supremely tender meat and elevates lesser cuts of meat, making it great for bottom round as well as the sirloin suggested here, which is for more of a special treat.

Serves 6

Beef:
1 tablespoon vegetable oil
3 lb sirloin roast
1 scant teaspoon English mustard powder
sea salt and freshly ground black pepper
1 heaping tablespoon grainy mustard

Preheat the oven to 300°F. Heat the oil in a large frying pan with a heatproof handle over high heat. Use a tea strainer or small sieve to dust the fat and underside of the roast with the mustard powder, and season it. Sear on all sides until golden—the ends, too—it should be well browned because you're roasting at a low temperature. Brush half the grainy mustard over the bottom of the meat with a pastry brush, and the rest over the top. Transfer the beef in the frying pan to the oven and roast for 50 minutes for rare, then remove from the oven, loosely cover with foil, and leave it to rest for 20 minutes. (I have a habit of forgetting that the handle of the pan is hot, so leaving a towel wrapped around it isn't a bad idea.) Thinly carve and serve with the gravy. The cold meat is also great sandwich material.
Carbohydrate 0.4g Protein 51.2g

GRAVY

For an even richer flavor, you could use a little Madeira or medium sherry in place of the same amount of red wine here.

Gravy:
2 tablespoons vegetable oil
4 cups mixture of diced onion, celery, carrot, and leek
2 garlic cloves, peeled and finely chopped
⅔ cup red wine
1⅔ cups beef stock

Heat the oil in a large saucepan over medium heat, add the vegetables, and cook for 30–35 minutes, stirring occasionally, until really well browned, almost black. Add the garlic a few minutes before the end, and then gradually pour in the red wine, and cook for a couple of minutes. Stir in the stock in two or three additions, add some seasoning, and simmer for about 5 minutes. Pass the gravy through a sieve, pressing out as much as possible from the vegetables. If it tastes at all thin, you can simmer it a few minutes longer, and check the seasoning. If you let it stand for any length of time, there may be a little oil on the surface, which you can skim off. Add any juices given out when you slice the beef.
Carbohydrate 5.2g Protein 52.3g

THICKENED GRAVY
If you want to thicken the gravy slightly, add 2 teaspoons **flour** to the pan after cooking the vegetables, then add the wine and cook, stirring, for a couple of minutes until it thickens.
Carbohydrate 6.5g Protein 52.5g

Roast beef with beets and horseradish sauce

Here the beef roasts in a relatively high oven, which is traditional, with lots of syrupy sweet onions and beets. The secret is to slice the beets thinly enough. The vegetables are quite good-natured and won't come to any harm if you need to cook the beef a little more or less, depending on the size of the roast and how you like it cooked.

Serves 4

1½ lbs beets, peeled and cut into
    thin wedges
4 tablespoons extra virgin olive oil
sea salt and freshly ground black
    pepper
4 red onions, peeled, halved, and
    thinly sliced
1¾ lbs bottom round or rump
    roast
1 tablespoon balsamic vinegar
⅓ cup coarsely chopped
    flat-leaf parsley

Preheat the oven to 400°F. For a 1¾ lb piece of meat, allow 30–40 minutes for the beef to leave it medium-rare to medium, and the beets will take 60–70 minutes in total. Arrange the beets in a large roasting pan (about 10 × 15 inches), pour in 2 tablespoons of olive oil, season, and toss, and cook for 20 minutes.

Scatter the onions over the beets, drizzle in another couple of tablespoons of oil, season, and give the vegetables a stir, then roast for another 10 minutes. At the same time, heat a large pan over high heat, season the beef, and sear to brown all over, starting with the fat side.

Drizzle the balsamic vinegar over the vegetables and give them a stir, nestle the beef fat-side up in the center, and roast for another 30–40 minutes or until a meat thermometer reads 125°F for medium-rare, and 140°F for medium after several minutes. Remove from the oven, loosely cover the pan with foil, and leave to rest for 15 minutes. Thinly carve the beef. Stir the parsley into the vegetables, and serve with the beef and the horseradish cream.
Carbohydrate 24.2g Protein 45.5g

WITH HORSERADISH CREAM
Blend ½ cup **low-fat crème fraîche** with 1–2 teaspoons of **horseradish** in a bowl and season with **sea salt**.
Carbohydrate 25.5g Protein 46.2g

Duck à l'orange

An oldie but a goodie, updated. It's easy to see why oranges are so often paired with duck, slicing through that louche richness. If the season allows, this is even better made with blood oranges.

Serves 4

Duck:
1 × 4½ lb oven-ready duck, untrussed, ideally with giblets
sea salt and freshly ground black pepper
⅔ cup orange juice
1 cup giblet or chicken stock
watercress, to serve

Roast onions:
4 red onions, peeled and cut into slim wedges
2 whole oranges, sliced, ends discarded
1 cinnamon stick
2 star anise
2 bay leaves
about 3–4 tablespoons rendered duck fat
duck liver (if included), fatty membranes removed and diced

Preheat the oven to 450°F. Pat the duck dry using paper towels, prick all over using the tip of a sharp knife, and season a little more generously than usual with salt, rubbing it into the skin. Place it breast side down on a roasting rack in a large roasting pan and roast for 1¾ hours. Drain off the fat after 1 hour (this can be used for roasting the onions), but without basting—you may find it easiest to transfer the duck and rack to a plate first—then turn the bird breast-side up.

At the end of roasting, place the duck on the rack over a large plate, pouring any juices inside the bird back into the pan, and leave to rest for 15 minutes. Drain the excess fat from the roasting pan, add the orange juice, and simmer to reduce by about half, scraping up all the sticky residue from the base of the pan. Add the stock and continue to simmer until nicely rich, then taste for seasoning. Carve and serve the duck with the gravy, watercress, and onions.
Carbohydrate 3.9g Protein 27.7g

Arrange the onions and orange slices in a large roasting pan with the spices and bay leaves. After an hour of cooking the duck, at the same time as you drain off the fat, drizzle 3 tablespoons of the fat over the onions and roast for 55–60 minutes (to include the resting time for the bird), stirring halfway through. If you happen to have the duck liver, then heat a teaspoon of the duck fat in a small frying pan over medium-high heat. Add the liver, season, and cook for about 1 minute to seal it on the outside, while leaving it rare within, tossing constantly. Serve this with over the onions, discarding the orange and aromatics.
Carbohydrate 19.9g Protein 31.4g

Slow-roast salt and pepper duck

Like Peking duck, this has everything to do with the delicate sheaths of crisp skin, so sprightly sautéed kale seem like the right accompaniment, but these aren't a must. It's a great way of cooking duck, whatever you want to serve it with. Two bunches of greens may provide a little more than you want, so bear in mind you can sauté it afterward with some root vegetables in all that lovely duck fat given out during the slow roasting.

Serves 4

Duck:
1 × 5-lb oven-ready duck, untrussed, ideally with giblets
sea salt and freshly ground black pepper
a handful each of fresh sage leaves and thyme sprigs
½ cup medium sherry
1⅔ cups giblet or chicken stock

Spring cabbage:
2 bunches of kale
extra virgin olive oil
freshly grated nutmeg

Preheat the oven to 325°F. Generously season the duck all over, rubbing the salt and pepper into the skin, and stuff the cavity with the herbs. Place the duck breast side up (ideally on a rack) in a roasting pan and roast for 3 hours, draining the fat into a bowl at roughly hourly intervals for the first couple of hours.

While the duck is roasting slice the greens across as finely as possible, discarding the tough stalks at the base. Give them a wash in a sink of cold water, and then a whirl in a salad spinner to dry them off.

Turn up the oven temperature to 425°F and roast the duck for another 15 minutes to color and crisp the skin. Remove from the oven and transfer the duck on the rack to a warm plate, tipping any juices back into the pan, and leave to rest for 15 minutes while you make the gravy and cook the greens.

Skim any excess fat from the roasting pan, add the sherry, and simmer for several minutes until it is well reduced, scraping up any sticky residue from the bottom. Add the stock, bring to a boil, and simmer for several minutes until rich and amalgamated, then season to taste and pour into a warm gravy boat.

At the same time cook the greens in batches. Heat either a tablespoon of the rendered duck fat or olive oil in a large pan over high heat, add a pile of the greens, season with salt and nutmeg, and sauté until they wilt and start to color, then remove them to a warm serving bowl and cook the remainder in the same way.

Carve the duck, or loosely pull it apart, making sure you get all of the skin—it should be crisp both top and bottom. Serve with the kale and gravy.
Carbohydrate 5.5g Protein 33.3g

THICKENED GRAVY
Stir in 1 tablespoon **flour** after adding the sherry and allow it to bubble momentarily, then gradually blend in the stock, and pass through a sieve into the gravy boat.
Carbohydrate 8.6g Protein 33.7g

Chile roast pork belly

All those lovely succulent strips of meat, the caramelized edges and crispy crackling…. This can be as indulgent or restrained as you choose—that is, you don't "have to" eat the fat or the crackling.

Serves 4

Marinade:
1 medium-hot red chile, core and
    seeds discarded
3 inches fresh ginger, peeled and
    cut up
4 garlic cloves, peeled
1 heaping teaspoon ground
    coriander
1 heaping teaspoon ground cumin
⅓ teaspoon cayenne pepper
1 tablespoon vegetable oil

Pork:
1 × 3-lb pork belly roast, preferably
    ribs-in, skin cut off and scored
    at ½-inch intervals
sea salt

Bok choy:
1 tablespoon vegetable oil
1 lb bok choy, base trimmed,
    cut into lengths an inch long
1 cup chicken stock

Put all the marinade ingredients in a food processor and process to a paste. Rub this into the pork on either side, at the ends, and into any crevices. Place the pork, ribs down, in a large roasting pan, cover, and chill for 1 hour.

Preheat the oven to 425°F. Season the pork on both sides with salt and pour a glass of water into the base of the pan. Place the skin rind-up in another roasting pan, again seasoning with salt. Roast the pork for 2 hours with the crackling below, turning down the oven temperature to 350°F after 30 minutes. Remove the pork from the oven and transfer to a warm plate to rest for 20 minutes, and turn the oven back up to 425°F to crisp the crackling for another 15–20 minutes.

Carve the pork between the ribs, halving the strips if long, and serve with the bok choy and gravy, and the crackling.
Carbohydrate 2.1g Protein 72.2g

WITH BOK CHOY
Place the roasting pan used for the pork over medium heat, add the oil, and cook the bok choy stems for a couple of minutes until glossy and starting to relax, then stir in the leaves, add the stock, and simmer for a couple of minutes, incorporating all the caramelized bits from the base of the pan.
Carbohydrate 4.9g Protein 75.6g

SIMPLY ROAST PORK
For an easy Sunday or weekday, a rolled pork shoulder is fine eating. I like to rub it with spices, which makes for particularly alluring and tasty golden edges. There is no need for gravy here, just some roast vegetables, perhaps a mash, or green salad.

Ask your butcher for the skin to be removed, and the **pork shoulder** to be rolled and tied. Rub the meat with a **spice blend** such as za'atar or a masala and season with **sea salt** and **black pepper**. Place the skin, rind side up, in a separate roasting pan and rub with salt. Roast the two for 15 minutes at 475°F, then reduce the temperature to 350°F, and continue to roast for 55–65 minutes per every two pounds or until the meat registers 165°F on a meat thermometer. Leave the crackling in the oven while the meat rests for 20 minutes. A 3-lb roast (weighed with the rind) will serve 4–6.
Carbohydrate 1.4g Protein 67.2g

Leg of lamb roasted with anchovies

The notion of anchovies with lamb seems unlikely, and yet there is no hint of these salty little fish by the time the meat is roasted—they simply add another dimension or depth to the flavor. A leg of lamb doesn't have to mean feeding a large number of people; a small one weighing about 3¾ lbs is perfect for four. At least, that is your weekday excuse.

Serves 4

Lamb:
1 leg of lamb (about 3¾ lbs), knuckle removed
4–5 salted anchovies, cut into ½-inch pieces
a handful of fresh thyme sprigs
extra virgin olive oil
sea salt and freshly ground black pepper

Zucchini:
4 small zucchini, ends discarded, thickly sliced diagonally
1 tablespoon lemon juice
1 garlic clove, peeled and crushed to a paste
a handful of mint leaves, torn

Preheat the oven to 475°F. Make small slits all over the lamb flesh using a sharp knife, then with the help of the tip of a teaspoon handle, insert a piece of anchovy into each one. Put the thyme sprigs in a roasting pan that will accommodate the lamb snugly. Drizzle some olive oil all over the lamb, season the lamb, and place, fat side up, on top of the thyme in the pan. Roast for 15 minutes, then turn down the oven temperature to 350°F and cook for another 16 minutes per pound for medium. Remove from the oven and leave the lamb to rest in a warm place for 15–20 minutes. Carve the lamb across the grain and serve with the zucchini.

While the lamb is cooking, heat a couple of tablespoons of oil in a large frying pan over medium-high heat, add the zucchini, season, and cook until colored on either side but remaining slightly crisp. Whisk the lemon juice with the garlic and some seasoning in a small bowl, then whisk in 3 tablespoons of oil. Pour this over the zucchini in a bowl, leave to cool for about 10 minutes, then mix in the mint. This can be served warm or at room temperature.
Carbohydrate 3.5g Protein 65.8g

Butterflied leg of lamb

The first time I ordered this cut in my local butcher in Normandy, the French term for "butterflied" escaped me, and I found myself directing the butcher cut by cut, like a surgeon overseeing an emergency operation. It is basically a leg that has been boned and opened out, and it cooks like a big juicy steak. It lends itself to being marinated and also barbecued. Weber kettles are fantastic for cooking large cuts—whole chickens, fish, and legs of lamb. Here I would allow 50–60 minutes for a 5-lb butterflied leg.

Serves 6

Marinade:
2 bay leaves, torn into pieces
1 teaspoon fresh thyme leaves
3 shallots, peeled and finely
   chopped
3 garlic cloves, peeled and crushed
   to a paste
3 tablespoons vegetable oil
3 tablespoons Calvados or brandy

Lamb:
1 butterflied leg of lamb
   (about 5 lbs)
sea salt and freshly ground black
   pepper

Combine all the marinade ingredients in a large bowl or roasting pan. Open out the butterflied leg of lamb, place it in the bowl or pan, and using your hands, coat both sides with the marinade. Cover it with plastic wrap and chill for several hours, or overnight.

Bring the leg back up to room temperature for 1 hour before cooking. Preheat the oven to 425°F. Season the marinated lamb on both sides and place it, fat side up, in a large roasting pan, opening it out. Roast for 10 minutes per pound—less than you would normally cook a leg for, to allow for the fact that it has been boned and opened out.

Baste the meat halfway through.

Remove the lamb from the oven and leave it to rest in a warm place for 20 minutes, then transfer it to a carving board. Skim the excess fat from the roasting pan—there should be plenty of juices—and heat to a simmer, scraping up all the sticky residue from the base of the pan, then add a drop of water to achieve a tasty jus. Slice the lamb across the grain, adding any juices given out as it rested to the gravy.

Carbohydrate 0.7g Protein 81.1g

Kleftiko

The romantic outward-bound origins of this dish lie with Greek bandits, who would slow-roast their stolen meat or *kleftiko* in a sealed hole in the ground, to conceal the sweet aromas of dinner cooking from their pursuers. And whatever happened in between, today it refers to lamb or goat cooked in a sealed parcel, and we love it for that reason alone. The lamb infuses with oregano and garlic as it roasts. Feta at the end is optional, but it does go particularly well with the lemon and herbs.

Serves 6

1 shoulder of lamb (about 4½ lbs)
extra virgin olive oil
sea salt and freshly ground black
    pepper
a small bunch of fresh oregano
¼ teaspoon ground cinnamon
2 heads of garlic, tops cut off and
    individual cloves separated
juice of 1 lemon
1 cup feta, diced (optional)

Preheat the oven to 275°F. Heat a large frying pan over medium-high heat. Using your hands, lightly coat the lamb with oil, season and sear to color it all over.

Now make a parcel by laying two long sheets of parchment paper one on top of the other at right angles. You want to allow enough spare at the ends to be able to pleat the edges together 2–3 times and leave a pocket of air within, once the lamb is inside. Pull off some of the oregano leaves and spread half the leaves and sprigs in the center of the paper. Drizzle on a little oil and place the lamb on top. Dust with cinnamon, sprinkle the remaining oregano leaves and sprigs, then scatter the garlic cloves over and around the lamb. Drizzle with more oil and the lemon juice and then seal the parcel by bringing the opposite sides to the center and pleating together. Place the parcel in a roasting pan and roast for 5 hours until the meat is meltingly tender.

If you are serving it with the feta, turn up the oven temperature to 425°F, open the paper at the top, sprinkle on the cheese, baste everything with the juices, and return to the oven for 10 minutes. Skim off any excess fat from the juices before serving.
Carbohydrate 1.9g Protein 53.4g

THE FISH SHOP

Fish fried in batter, fishcakes with more potato than fish, AND coated in bread crumbs, a pie with butter, cream, tiny bit of fish, and lots of mashed potatoes, and fries, fries, and more fries. Personally, because I've never eaten fried food, I find the idea of it offputting. I remember my son telling my mother, when he was about twelve, that he had never had fish and chips. You would have thought from her reaction that I had committed some terrible crime: "Poor child, you poor, poor child." And she swore to correct it on our very next visit, which she did, and then proceeded to order in fish and chips almost every time we went to see her. It wasn't that I hadn't ever given him fish and chips on principle; I just don't particularly like it, so it had never occurred to me.

And I do think that if you change your eating habits for a healthier regime, eventually you go off the foods you have left behind. A sweet tooth recedes once you give up sugar in your tea or coffee, and if you are unaccustomed to eating store-bought milk chocolate and cookies, they are unpalatably overwhelming.

So part of the journey is about accepting this shift. These dishes may not convince the diehard who will only settle for the original dish, but approach them with an open mind and accept them as being delicious in their own right, and there is plenty of fine feasting to be done.

The ultimate shrimp cocktail

However hackneyed—and over the years it has been abused more than most dishes—shrimp cocktail never dates. Well made, it is a gorgeous big splash of an affair, in which very finely sliced chilled lettuce is layered with shrimp and a homemade cocktail sauce. Restaurants like the Wolseley in London keep the flame alive with their ice-cold silvered cocktail dishes filled to the brim (they do crab and lobster too—just as good), and this recipe is very much based on their tradition.

Serves 4

Cocktail sauce:
1 large organic egg yolk
1 scant teaspoon Dijon mustard
⅓ cup vegetable oil
1 tablespoon ketchup
a shake or two of Tabasco sauce

Vinaigrette:
1 teaspoon Dijon mustard
sea salt and freshly ground black
    pepper
3 tablespoons vegetable oil
1 teaspoon lemon juice

Shrimp:
1 lb medium shrimp, cooked
    and peeled
a generous squeeze of lemon juice
2 tablespoons finely chopped
    flat-leaf parsley, plus a little
    extra to serve
1 Iceberg lettuce, chilled, base
    trimmed
3 slim scallions, trimmed and
    finely sliced

To prepare the sauce, whisk the egg yolk with the mustard in a medium bowl, then gradually whisk in the oil, a few drops at a time to begin with, until the mayonnaise takes. Stir in the ketchup, then season with Tabasco; I like a noticeable nip of chile.

To make the vinaigrette, whisk the mustard with a little seasoning in a medium bowl, then whisk in the oil a tablespoon at a time, until it is thick and mayonnaise-like. Stir in the lemon juice and then 2–4 teaspoons of water to thin the vinaigrette to the consistency of cream.

Toss the shrimp in a bowl with a generous squeeze of lemon, a little black pepper, and the parsley. Quarter the lettuce downward, then halve each quarter across and slice as finely as possible into grasslike strands using a sharp knife. Combine this in another bowl with the scallions, and toss with the vinaigrette.

Divide half the lettuce among four deep bowls or sundae glasses, add half the shrimp, drizzle a teaspoon of the cocktail sauce over each one, and repeat the layers, then sprinkle with a little more parsley. *Carbohydrate 3.4g Protein 24.4g*

SPEEDY COCKTAIL SAUCE
You can also make a speedy low-fat cocktail sauce with 1 cup **sour cream**, 1 tablespoon **mayonnaise**, 1 tablespoon **ketchup,** and a little **sea salt**. *Carbohydrate 5.4g Protein 25g*

Salade Niçoise

There is something about a Salade Niçoise that gives you the same kind of feeling of being as satiated as if had you eaten a steak. Perhaps not suprisingly, as the combination of tuna, eggs, and olives is a cocktail of superfoods. On a hungry day, a can of tuna, which can be dressed up with a squeeze of lemon, some chopped parsley, and finely sliced chile, is a blessing of a high-protein snack.

Given the number of pantry ingredients this calls for, it makes a regular appearance in our house, not least because fresh tuna is off the menu on sustainable grounds, so jars of sustainable Albacore that promise big meaty flakes of pinkish ivory fish are a great luxury fall-back. Spanish delis also make a good hunting ground for tuna that is a cut above the norm.

Serves 4

4 large eggs
6 tablespoons extra virgin olive oil
1½ tablespoons lemon juice
sea salt and freshly ground black
     pepper
2 tablespoons small capers
     (eg nonpareille), rinsed
2 × 7oz jars or cans of tuna in
     spring water, drained
4 salted anchovy fillets, halved
     lengthwise
3 ripe plum or heirloom tomatoes,
     cores removed, cut into wedges
½ cup pitted green or black olives
4 cups arugula

Bring a medium pan of water to a boil, add the eggs, and boil for 7–8 minutes to leave them slightly wet in the center, then drain and cool in cold water.

Whisk the olive oil, lemon juice, some seasoning, and the capers in a large deep salad bowl, one that gives you enough room for tossing once you have layered all the ingredients. Dry the tuna on a double thickness of paper towels, then break it into chunks or coarse flakes. Add to the dressing, and turn to coat everything. Lay the anchovy fillets on top, then the tomatoes and finally the olives. Finally pile the arugula on top. Cover with plastic wrap and set aside in a cool place.

To serve, shell and quarter the eggs. Gently turn the salad over a couple of times, and arrange the eggs on top.
Carbohydrate 2.9g Protein 25g

Whole mackerel roasted with cherry tomatoes and olives

We are inclined to give this fish the northerly treatment by marrying it with sharp fruit sauces like rhubarb or coating it in oatmeal, but it is equally at home with sunnier fare like tomatoes on the vine, olives, arugula, and balsamic vinegar. It does, after all, has something in common with sardines—in fact, pretty much any way that you might cook sardines will also translate to mackerel.

Serves 4

4 × whole mackerel (about 10oz each), cleaned
extra virgin olive oil
sea salt and freshly ground black pepper
1 lb cherry tomatoes on the vine
1 tablespoon balsamic vinegar
1 cup pitted black olives
4 large handfuls of arugula

Preheat the oven to 475°F. Score the mackerel flesh diagonally at 1½-inch intervals on both sides, brush with oil, and season. Heat a large, nonstick frying pan over medium-high heat and sear the mackerel, one at a time, for 1 minute on each side, then arrange them head to tail in a roasting pan. Lay the tomatoes on top, drizzle on 2 tablespoons of oil and the balsamic vinegar, and roast for 15 minutes. Add the olives on top and leave to stand for 5 minutes. Serve with any juices spooned over. Pile some arugula on top or to the side of each mackerel and drizzle over a little more oil.
Carbohydrate 5.4g Protein 44.4g

SIMPLY MACKEREL FILLETS
Mackerel fillets are a great dinner basic, loaded with goodness and all those fish oils, and they only take around 5 minutes to cook. One of my favorite ways of eating these is to dress some cooked and diced beets with olive oil and balsamic vinegar, throw in a little chopped dill, and pile this on top of watercress.

Heat a teaspoon of **extra virgin olive oil** in a large, nonstick frying pan over medium heat. Season around 1½ lbs **mackerel fillets** (ideally 4) on both sides, and cook in two batches, skin-side down, for about 3 minutes, until golden and crispy and the flesh is cooked through by about two-thirds, then turn and cook for 1 minute longer on the flesh side. Tranfer these to a plate and cook the rest in the same way. *Carbohydrate 0g Protein 28.1g*

Moules marinière

Moules Marinière is at heart an elementary dish, and it's a sign of the times that we tend to trick it up—it's more unusual to encounter the original than some fusion take on it. But the original is by far and away still the best, especially if you happen to be eating it in the environs of mussel beds, something my family is spoiled with at our house in Normandy, because an extensive marine reserve fringes our coastline.

At the beachside restaurant La Cale, in Blainville-sur-Mer, from where this recipe derives, there will be about five pots on the go at any one time, with the waiting table's number written in magic marker on the lid. The fries they serve with them are about the only sort that I am ever tempted to eat—and do—skinny and crisp with hundreds of deliciously crunchy splinters of potato. But here we will do without.

Serves 2

4 lbs fresh mussels
3 tablespoons vegetable oil
2 tablespoons very finely chopped onion
2 tablespoons very finely chopped shallot
1 garlic clove, peeled and finely chopped
½ cup white wine
⅓ cup low-fat crème fraîche
a handful coarsely chopped flat-leaf parsley

Give the mussels a good wash in a sink of cold water, discarding any that are broken or that do not close when tapped. Pull off any beards and scrape off any barnacles. If very dirty, give them a second rinse.

Heat the oil in a large saucepan over high heat, add the onion, shallot, and garlic, and cook for about 1 minute until softened, then pour in the wine and simmer to reduce by half. Add the mussels, put on the lid, and cook for 5–6 minutes until opened. Stir in the crème fraîche and parsley and serve at once. *Carbohydrate 13.5g Protein 33.6g*

Salmon, shrimp, and tomato stew

This delicous stew was designed with accessibility in mind, given that so often fish stews require hunting for the right species, but the caveat is that they should be responsibly farmed. You can also use scallops here in place of salmon, their gristle removed, in which case halve the quantity and the poaching time.

Serves 4

1 lb plum tomatoes
2 tablespoons extra virgin olive oil
5 shallots, peeled, halved, and sliced
1 celery heart, trimmed and sliced
2 teaspoons finely chopped
    medium-hot red chile
sea salt
a large pinch of saffron filaments,
    (about 20)
1¼ cups fish stock
1 lb salmon fillet, skinned and cut
    into 1-inch pieces
½ lb raw peeled shrimp
coarsely chopped flat-leaf parsley,
    to serve

Bring a medium pan of water to a boil, cut out the core from the top of each tomato, dunk them into boiling water for 20 seconds and then into cold water. Slip off the skins and coarsely chop them.

Heat the oil in a large saucepan over medium heat and cook the shallots for several minutes until softened. Add the celery and chile and cook for another 5–7 minutes until glossy and relaxed.

Add the tomatoes and some salt and cook for about 8 minutes, pressing the tomatoes down until you have a textured purée. Add the saffron and the fish stock, bring to a boil, and simmer over low heat for 10 minutes. The stew can be prepared to this point in advance.

To serve, bring the stock base back to a boil. Season the salmon and add to the pan, together with the shrimp, and poach for 5 minutes. Serve the stew scattered with chopped parsley.
Carbohydrate 5.4g Protein 33.6g

Cod, crayfish, spinach, and cilantro stew

This has Portuguese aspirations with its dark green spinach leaves, tender lily-white cod, and snippets of bacon, and the wild card of lots of fresh cilantro. But as with any fish stew, the fish is merely a suggestion: cod can mean anything white and meaty, the more obscure and less sought-after the better.

Serves 6

3 tablespoons unsalted butter

3 large onions, peeled, quartered, and thinly sliced across

sea salt and freshly ground black pepper

⅓ cup white wine

3¾ cups chicken stock

1 lb spinach leaves, sliced if large

3 cups cilantro leaves and fine stems, coarsely chopped, plus extra to serve

1 teaspoon vegetable oil

6 slices unsmoked bacon, diced

1⅓ lbs cod (skinned weight), cut into 1-inch dice

10oz cooked and peeled crayfish or large shrimp

Melt the butter in a large saucepan over lowish heat, add the onions, sprinkle with a teaspoon of salt, and cook for 15–20 minutes, stirring occasionally, until soft and syrupy without allowing them to color more than a little. Add the wine, turn up the heat, and cook to reduce it by half. Pour in the chicken stock and bring to a boil, then add the spinach, half the cilantro, and some seasoning. Bring the stock back to a boil, then cover the pan and cook over low heat for 10 minutes, stirring the stock after a couple of minutes to submerge the leaves.

Briefly chop two-thirds of the vegetables in a food processor to break them up, then return these to the pan. The stew can be prepared to this point in advance.

Shortly before serving, heat the oil in a large, nonstick frying pan over medium heat and cook the bacon for 5–7 minutes until lightly golden, stirring frequently and separating out the pieces, then drain on a double thickness of paper towels. Bring the stock base back to a boil, add the cod, cover, and simmer for 2 minutes. Add the crayfish or shrimp, half the bacon, and the remaining cilantro, and cook for 1 minute longer. Serve the stew sprinkled with extra cilantro and the remaining bacon.

Carbohydrate 11.9g Protein 40.2g

Baked cod, beets, and mint

Cod and beets make a classic northerly marriage, but roasting invites in a little sunshine, here with caramelized onions, garlic, and orange.

Serves 4

finely grated zest of 1 orange
**2 garlic cloves, peeled and crushed
    to a paste**
6 tablespoons extra virgin olive oil
**1⅓ lbs cod (skinned weight),
    cut into 8 pieces**
1½ lbs beets
**2 red onions, peeled, halved, and
    sliced across**
**sea salt and freshly ground black
    pepper**

Blend the orange zest and garlic with 3 tablespoons of oil in a large bowl, add the cod, and stir to coat it, then cover and chill for 1 hour.

Preheat the oven to 475°F. Without peeling the beets, trim the tops and bottoms of shoots and roots, and cut into wedges. Arrange these in a large roasting pan (about 10 × 15 inches) with the onions, pour in 3 tablespoons of olive oil, and season. Cover with foil and roast for 30 minutes, then uncover, stir the vegetables, and roast for another 25 minutes.

Five minutes before the end of this time, heat a large, nonstick frying pan over high heat, and season and sear the pieces of cod in two batches for 30 seconds on either side to lightly color them. Stir the vegetables and tuck the fish in between, and return to the oven for 5 minutes.
Carbohydrate 18.8g Protein 31.4g

WITH MINT SAUCE
You may not need all of this sauce, but it makes a lovely dip for crudités, too.

While the dish is cooking, blend together 1 cup **sour cream**, 2 heaping tablespoons finely chopped **mint**, 1½ teaspoons **Dijon mustard**, and a pinch of **sea salt** in a medium bowl. Serve this spooned on top of the fish and vegetables, with a little extra mint scattered over.
Carbohydrate 21.2g Protein 33.2g

Roast lemon sole with sage and onions

Lemon sole is a hugely underrated fish, as sweet and delicate as Dover sole but more down-to-earth. Here the fish are roasted whole with sage leaves and onion.

Serves 2

2 × lemon sole (about 14oz), cleaned
3 tablespoons salted butter, melted
sea salt and freshly ground black pepper
1 red onion, peeled, halved, and finely sliced
a large handful of fresh sage leaves
⅔ cup white wine

Preheat the oven to 425°F. Score the fish flesh diagonally at 1½ inch intervals on both sides, then brush with the melted butter and season. Heat a large, nonstick frying pan over medium-high heat, and sear the fish, one at a time, first for 1 minute on the upper side, and then another minute on the lower side, and slide out into a large roasting pan (about 10 × 15 inches). Add the rest of the melted butter to the pan then the onion and sage leaves, and cook for a few minutes, stirring frequently, until just starting to color. Spoon this over the fish, pour the wine into the bottom of the pan, and roast for 15 minutes. I would let everyone bone their own fish, and serve with the juices spooned over.
Carbohydrate 10.6g Protein 50.9g

Grilled squid with lemon and chile

The secret to grilling squid is to get your grill pan really, really, really hot so that it brands the flesh.

Serves 2
Squid:
1 lb squid, about the length of your hand
arugula, or a mixture of salad leaves containing arugula

Sauce and dressing:
1 tablespoon lemon juice, plus an extra squeeze for the salad
½ teaspoon finely grated lemon zest
1 medium-hot red chile, core and seeds discarded, and finely chopped
sea salt and freshly ground black pepper
2 tablespoons extra virgin olive oil, plus extra for squid and salad

First, the task of cleaning your squid. Tug the tentacles away from the pouch to separate them. Pull off the wings and with them the transparent film covering the pouch, and discard. Remove the hard pen from inside and as much of the insides as you can. Slit the pouch open from top to bottom, open it out, and scrape off any residual white matter. Score the flesh in a criss-cross pattern at ½-inch intervals using the sharp tip of a knife, and set aside. Cut the tentacles off the body just above the eyes. Rinse and pat dry.

Preheat your grill pan on high heat. Make the sauce by whisking together the tablespoon of lemon juice and the zest, chile, and some salt, then add the oil. Put the salad leaves in a bowl and toss with olive oil to coat them, then add a squeeze of lemon and the smallest sprinkling of salt.

Brush the squid on both sides with the oil, season, and cook for 3 minutes in total, turning it halfway through. As you cook the second side, the pieces should curl up and be striped with gold on the outside. Serve the squid with the sauce spooned over, accompanied by the salad.
Carbohydrate 3.7g Protein 24.6g

Salad of grilled salmon with pickled vegetables

This is a slightly unusual dish in that it combines grilled salmon with lightly pickled vegetables. As an all-in-one dish, it has lots going for it—fish with a salad and dressing. It can be made several hours or even a day in advance. You can also pad it out with other salads; tomato would be good.

Serves 6

Pickled vegetables:
2 tablespoons extra virgin olive oil
1 teaspoon salt
⅔ cup dry white wine
1½ tablespoons white wine vinegar
2 slim carrots, trimmed, peeled, and thinly sliced
1 leek, trimmed and thinly sliced
1⅓ cups small (¾-inch) cauliflower florets
2 bay leaves
3 garlic cloves, peeled and smashed
a large pinch of saffron filaments, (about 20)
a pinch of red pepper flakes
½ teaspoon sugar

Salmon:
6 × 5oz salmon fillets, skin on
extra virgin olive oil
sea salt and freshly ground black pepper

Put all the pickled vegetables ingredients into a medium saucepan with ⅔ cup water, bring to a boil, and simmer for about 20 minutes (ensure the vegetables are submerged), until everything is tender.

Meanwhile, heat a large nonstick frying pan over medium heat. Brush the salmon fillets with olive oil and season on both sides. You will need to cook them in batches. Cook for 4–6 minutes, skin side down, until golden and you can see from the sides that the fish is cooked at least halfway through. Turn and cook the flesh side for 1–2 minutes, leaving the fish slightly underdone in the center; it should still give a little if you press it.

Arrange the fillets skin side up in a shallow dish that holds them fairly snugly, but with a little space in between. Stir 2 tablespoons of oil into the hot vegetable mixture, and pour it over the fish, which should be covered by about two-thirds. Loosely cover with plastic wrap or foil and leave to cool completely for about 3 hours. The dish can be made up to a day in advance, in which case chill the cooled fish and vegetables and bring back to room temperature an hour before eating.
Carbohydrate 4.8g Protein 31.7g

Crispy salmon and cabbage

Cabbage is potentially a brute of a vegetable, but slice it wafer-fine into a mass of grasslike strands and cook rather than boil it and it is reborn. The bacon brings out the flavor of the salmon, but you could leave it out, and yes, you could leave out the sauce as well; if you're simply after a quickie supper, salmon with cabbage is an austere delight.

Serves 6

Salmon:
1 tablespoon extra virgin olive oil
finely grated zest of 1 lemon
6 × 5oz salmon fillets, skin on

Cabbage:
3 tablespoons unsalted butter
5oz unsmoked bacon, diced
1 small white cabbage, outer leaves
    discarded, quartered, core
    removed, and finely sliced
1 small Savoy cabbage, outer leaves
    discarded, quartered, core
    removed, and finely sliced
sea salt and freshly ground black
    pepper

Preheat the oven to 400°F. Combine the oil and lemon zest in a small bowl, and rub all over the salmon fillets on a plate then set aside for 15 minutes.

Heat half the butter in a large saucepan over medium-high heat, add the bacon, and cook for 5–6 minutes, stirring frequently until it starts to color, then add half the cabbage and cook for about 4 minutes until wilted but still crisp, seasoning it with black pepper halfway through. Transfer this to a bowl and cook the remaining cabbage in the same way. Return all the cabbage to the pan.

At the same time as cooking the cabbage, heat a large, nonstick frying pan over medium-high heat, and season the salmon fillets on both sides. You will probably need to cook them in two batches. First color the skin for 4–5 minutes, then turn and sear the flesh for 30 seconds, then transfer them to a roasting pan skin side up, spaced a little way apart. Roast for 6–8 minutes— you can slip a knife through the center of the thickest fillet to see if it is done; it should be faintly translucent, just cooked.

Reheat the cabbage if necessary, and serve as a bed for the salmon.
Carbohydrate 7.5g Protein 37.4g

WITH MUSTARD CREAM
A luxurious touch for the salmon and cabbage; any left over is delicious with roast beef.

Blend together ⅔ cup **sour cream**, 1½ teaspoons **grainy mustard** and 2 teaspoons finely chopped **tarragon** together in a bowl. Cover and chill until required. Serve spooned over the salmon and cabbage.
Carbohydrate 8.5g Protein 38.2g

Shopping with care

As addictions go, there could be worse—I eat salmon seasoned with Maldon sea salt and black pepper then fried until crisp in its own oil, several days of the week.

In fact, sometimes for breakfast. I always felt slightly embarrassed about eating it so early when all around me were on toast and oatmeal, until I encountered a Japanese breakfast menu in a London hotel where Salmon Teriyaki came with pickled plums, and I have been indulging at that time of day ever since. It is an addiction that has been with me all of my life—my husband and I always say that the reason we knew I was pregnant with our first child was because on a visit to the beautiful Tuscan hill town of Montepulciano, instead of choosing a restaurant for its local specialties, I made him traipse around the town looking at menus until he could find one with salmon, such was my craving.

Wild Atlantic salmon was already endangered by the time my habit took hold, so I don't see farmed salmon as being second best; I actively like its softer texture and buttery oiliness. It's delicate and nourishing and leaves you satiated in a particular way. But, there are environmental concerns over intensive salmon farming, and to eat responsibly, we need either to buy organic farmed salmon or that from sustainable farms. I still believe, however, that in the long term, if the ecological issues can be resolved, farming has to hold the key to taking pressure off wild stocks. It is a comparatively new and emergent industry, so at the same time as applying pressure, I don't think we should be giving up on it. Simply be prepared to pay more for less intensively reared premium brands.

For protein lovers, salmon is one of the most versatile of fish, a great ingredient to have a supply of cooked in the fridge, as good eaten cold as hot, since its texture remains unchanged. It is readily turned into a delicious salad with fine green beans, capers, lemon juice, and olive oil, or served with a big green salad with avocado. And it has the edge over smoked salmon, which comes loaded with salt.

Simply fried salmon

I tend to cook my salmon in my largest nonstick saucepan rather than a frying pan, because of the tedium of cleaning up the minute particles of oil that are given off as the fish fries. Alternatively you can cover a frying pan with a lid, leaving a small gap.

Heat a large nonstick frying pan or saucepan over medium heat, season the top (i.e. flesh) side of thick, skinned **salmon fillets** weighing about 5 ounces each with **sea salt** and **freshly ground black pepper**, and cook, top side down, for about 5 minutes until golden and crispy and you can see the fillets have cooked through by a third to half, then turn and cook the other side for about 3 minutes—exact timings will depend on the thickness of the fillet, but it should have just lost its translucency in the center.
Carbohydrate 0g Protein 30.3g

Whole roast salmon stuffed with herbs

If you are planning on cooking for a group, roasting a small whole salmon makes more sense than cooking fillets; any left over has nearly as many uses as cold roast chicken, and it offers the same ease of cooking. Even though we have salmon throughout the year, quite often there is an abundance during the summer, when fish this size abound. You can also make this using sea bass, in which case it may need another 5 minutes cooking.

Serves 4

1 × 11-lb whole salmon (preferably organic), gutted and scaled, head and tail removed
sea salt and freshly ground black pepper
4 tablespoons mixture of coarsely chopped fresh dill, flat-leaf parsley, and basil
⅓ cup white wine
5 tablespoons unsalted butter
1 tablespoon small capers, rinsed

Preheat the oven to 425°F and preheat the broiler. Score the salmon flesh diagonally on both sides at 2-inch intervals and season it with salt and pepper, as well as inside the cavity. Stuff herbs into the slashes, sprinkling any left over inside the cavity. Line a baking dish or pan that is as long as the salmon with a double layer of foil and lay the fish on top. Broil the salmon for 3–6 minutes on each side until the skin blisters and colors.

Cup the edges of the foil. Pour the wine over the salmon, dot with the butter, and roast for 25–30 minutes. Check whether it is cooked after 25 minutes by slipping a sharp knife between the backbone and the flesh. One should come away from the other with ease; if the flesh clings to the bones it needs a little longer.

Pour the juices into a bowl and stir in the capers. Fillet the salmon and serve with the caper butter spooned over.
Carbohydrate 2.2g Protein 61.7g

Salmon pie with minted zucchini

A fish pie is one of the great challenges for the low-carb cook—they are potentially as high in fat and carbs as any dish can be and are suitably luxurious eating. But equally, it is good to know that you can make a fabulous pie, reformed in its ways, and this one comes as a breath of fresh air—fish stewlike in its appeal with thin light juices. I would serve it with a garlic mayonnaise, and a vegetable mash is also welcome. Because there is no potato or béchamel, it's also good eaten cold.

Serves 6

Salmon:
2 lbs skinned salmon fillet,
    cut into 1½-inch pieces
½ cup white wine
sea salt and freshly ground black
    pepper

Sauce:
extra virgin olive oil
4 shallots, peeled and thinly sliced
2 garlic cloves, peeled and finely
    chopped
1 teaspoon finely chopped
    medium-hot red chile
1 × 14oz can chopped tomatoes
1 bay leaf
½ lb cooked and peeled shrimp
¾ cup pitted or stuffed green olives
a handful of fresh mint leaves
4 medium zucchini, ends trimmed
    and finely sliced*
garlic mayonnaise, to serve

Place the salmon pieces in a large saucepan, pour in the wine, and season with salt and pepper. Bring the liquid to a boil, then cover and cook over medium-low heat for 4–5 minutes until the salmon is just cooked through—don't worry if a few patches still seem a little translucent. Reserving the cooking liquid, remove the salmon using a slotted spoon, trying not to break it up, and transfer to a large bowl. Set aside while you make the sauce.

Heat a couple of tablespoons of oil in a medium saucepan over medium heat and cook the shallots for a couple of minutes, stirring frequently, until translucent and starting to color. Stir in the garlic and chile and continue to cook momentarily until fragrant. Add the tomatoes and fish cooking liquid, including any given out by the salmon as it rests, the bay leaf, and some seasoning. Bring to a boil, then cook over low heat for 20–30 minutes until the sauce reduces to a thick purée and the oil separates out, stirring and keeping a watchful eye toward the end of this time.

Carefully spoon the salmon into a 14-inch oval gratin dish or one of equivalent size, discarding any additional liquid that has been released while it rested. Scatter the shrimp and the olives over and between the salmon pieces. Discard the bay leaf and spoon the sauce over the fish, coating it as evenly as possible. You can prepare the pie to this point in advance, in which case allow it to cool, then cover and chill.

Preheat the oven to 400°F. Blend the mint to a purée with 4 tablespoons of olive oil, then toss this with the zucchini and some seasoning in a large bowl, separating out the slices to evenly coat them. Arrange in an even layer to cover the fish, drizzle with another couple of tablespoons of oil, and bake for 40–45 minutes until the top slices are patched with gold. Now heat the broiler and pop the pie under to color it more. Serve in shallow bowls, accompanied by garlic mayonnaise.
Carbohydrate 5.6g Protein 41.5g

TIP: The quickest route here is to use the slicing attachment on a food processor.

Fish and chips with tartare sauce

Here we have homemade fish sticks, lightly coated in ground almonds in place of bread crumbs, and oven-roasted fries that rely on celeriac rather than potato. You could get out the ketchup, but my own weakness is for tartare sauce.

This one's on my desert island list: just think of all those freshly caught fish cooked over an open fire—all you need for perfection is some mayonnaise laced with capers and cornichons.

Serves 4

Fish sticks:
1 cup almond flour
1½ teaspoons sea salt
⅓ teaspoon cayenne pepper
1–2 large eggs, beaten
1 lb skinned white fish fillets,
    ¾ inch thick, cut into sticks an
    inch wide and 2½ inches long
extra virgin olive oil
lemon wedges, to serve

2¾ lbs celeriac, skin cut off
finely grated zest of 1 lemon
    (optional), plus 1 tablespoon
    lemon juice
2 tablespoons extra virgin olive oil
2 tablespoons unsalted butter
sea salt and freshly ground black
    pepper

1 level teaspoon grainy mustard
1 level tablespoon finely chopped
    pickle
1 level tablespoon finely chopped
    capers
1 heaping tablespoon finely
    chopped flat-leaf parsley
⅔ cup mayonnaise

Combine the almond flour, salt, and cayenne pepper in a shallow bowl, and put the egg in a second shallow bowl. Dip the fish sticks first into the egg and then into the almond flour mixture and set aside on a plate. Heat a couple of tablespoons of oil in a large, nonstick frying over medium heat and cook the coated fish in batches for about 2 minutes on the first side until golden, and for 1–2 minutes on the second side, scraping out any burned crumbs between batches and replenishing the oil as necessary. Drain on a double thickness of paper towels, and serve with lemon wedges. You can also accompany them with celeriac fries and a teaspoon of tartare sauce, in which case a bowl of lettuce provides light relief.
Carbohydrate 1.5g Protein 22.3g

WITH CELERIAC FRIES

Preheat the oven to 425°F. Slice the celeriac ½ inch thick, then cut the slices into evenly sized fries—halve them if long. Arrange these in a large roasting pan (about 10 × 15 inches) with the lemon zest if you like a particularly lemony flavor. Drizzle with the olive oil and the lemon juice and give the vegetables a stir. Dot with the butter, season, and roast for 50–60 minutes, stirring the fries every 20 minutes by loosening them with a spatula.
Carbohydrate 8.7g Protein 26g

WITH TARTARE SAUCE

I think pretty much everything tastes great with tartare sauce; it is lovely with the fishcakes on page 152 as well.

Stir all the ingredients together in a bowl, cover, and chill until required.
Carbohydrate 9g Protein 26.2g

Shrimp and pepper tagine

This tagine is light and delicate, with fresh ginger replacing the usual dried spices. And it is relatively dry, compared to many Moroccan stews, making it good for eating with vegetable accompaniments. I like to cook the shrimp shell-on and peel them as I eat, but you could use raw peeled shrimp if you prefer.

Serves 4

a large pinch of saffron filaments, (about 20)

4 red peppers

4 plum tomatoes

3 tablespoons extra virgin olive oil

1 lb unpeeled raw large shrimp

4 garlic cloves, peeled and sliced

1 medium-hot red chile, seeds and membranes discarded, and finely sliced

1 teaspoon finely grated fresh ginger

½ teaspoon turmeric

sea salt

a squeeze of lemon juice

4 tablespoons coarsely chopped cilantro, to serve

Pour a tablespoon of boiling water over the saffron filaments in a small bowl and leave to infuse.

Preheat the oven to 425°F and roast the peppers on the oven rack for 15 minutes until the skin has blistered and started to color. Transfer them to a bowl, cover with plastic wrap, and leave to cool. Working over the bowl to capture the juices, slip off the skins, remove the seeds, and slice the flesh into thin strips.

Bring a small saucepan of water to a boil, cut out the core from the top of each tomato, plunge into the boiling water for 20 seconds and then into a bowl of cold water. Remove and slip off the skins, and cut each tomato into 6–8 wedges.

Heat the olive oil in a large saucepan or cast-iron casserole over medium-high heat, add the shrimp, and sauté on both sides until they turn from blue to pink. Transfer them to a bowl. Add the garlic, chile, and ginger to the pan and stir for about 30 seconds until nicely fragrant. Stir in the turmeric, add the tomatoes, and cook for a minute or two, mashing them down, then add the peppers, saffron water, pepper juices, and some salt, cover and cook over low heat for 10 minutes.

Give the sauce a stir, mashing the tomatoes to a coarse purée. Stir the shrimp into the sauce, cover, and cook for another 5–6 minutes until the shrimp feel firm when pressed. Season with a generous squeeze of lemon and taste for salt. Serve sprinkled with cilantro.

Carbohydrate 13.5g Protein 12.3g

Poached trout with cucumber and dill sauce

Hugely under-rated, trout is a worthy alternative to salmon and just as adaptable. If you want to serve it hot, allow the court-bouillon to cool, pour it over the vinegared fish, and place over medium–high heat. The moment any bubbles present themselves on the surface, turn the heat down low and poach for 5 minutes. Here you could dress the trout with a fine drizzle of warm, melted salty butter, lemon juice, some sea salt and freshly ground black pepper. Hot or cold, I would serve the trout with watercress.

Serves 4

Court-bouillon:
2 carrots, trimmed, peeled, and sliced
2 celery ribs, sliced
1 onion, peeled and chopped
1 bay leaf
a few parsley stalks
2 cups white wine

Trout:
4 × trout (about 8oz each), cleaned
⅔ cup white wine vinegar
3 tablespoons coarse sea salt

2 tablespoons extra virgin olive oil
4 shallots, peeled and finely chopped
1 cucumber, peeled, quartered, seeded, and diced
sea salt and freshly ground black pepper
4 tablespoons chopped dill, plus a little extra
1½ cups fat-free Greek yogurt
a squeeze of lemon juice

You will need to start preparing the trout several hours in advance of eating. Put the vegetables and herbs for the court-bouillon in a medium saucepan with the wine and 2 cups of water. Bring to a boil, cover, and simmer over low heat for 30 minutes.

Toward the end of this time, arrange the fish top to tail on their sides in a 12-inch oval cast-iron casserole. Bring the vinegar to a boil in a small saucepan with the salt, stirring until it dissolves, and pour evenly over the fish—any slime coating them should turn a grayish blue. Now pour the hot court-bouillon over the fish, bring it back to a healthy boil over medium-high heat, then cover, remove from heat, and leave to cool for several hours. Carefully lift the fish out of the court-bouillon onto plates to serve, dabbing any liquid that seeps out with paper towels.
Carbohydrate 11.5g Protein 36.3g

WITH CUCUMBER AND DILL SAUCE

Dill is particularly good with fish, and with cucumber, but should the fresh fronds prove hard to track down, chives would be next best.

Heat the olive oil in a large frying pan over medium heat and cook the shallots for 1–2 minutes, stirring occasionally, until softened without coloring. Add the cucumber, season, and cook for a few minutes longer, again stirring occasionally. Transfer the vegetables to a bowl, stir in the dill, and leave to cool. You can prepare the sauce to this point a couple of hours in advance. Shortly before serving, stir in the Greek yogurt and a squeeze of lemon juice, and taste for seasoning. Serve with the fish, sprinkling with a little extra dill.
Carbohydrate 16.2g Protein 44.7g

Fishcakes

A good fishcake is a suppertime staple, and these ones have passed the teenager litmus test. This involves the small white lie of not informing them it is celeriac instead of potato—and they didn't even suspect. Any fresh white fish fillets will be good here, but frequently frozen turn out fresher.

Serves 6

1⅓ lbs celeriac, skin cut off, cut into chunks
1 lb skinless white fish fillets, (cod, haddock, hake, etc)
½ cup white wine
2 tablespoons unsalted butter
sea salt and freshly ground black pepper
1 teaspoon anchovy paste (optional)
2 tablespoons capers, rinsed and chopped
1 large egg, beaten
12 slices bacon (smoked or unsmoked)
a little vegetable oil

Bring a medium saucepan of salted water to a boil, add the celeriac, and simmer for 15–20 minutes until tender. At the same time, arrange the fish fillets in a single layer on the base of another medium pan. Pour in the wine, dot with the butter, and season them. Bring the wine to a boil, then cover the pan and cook over low heat for 5–6 minutes. Transfer the fish to a plate using a spatula, and leave it to rest for 10 minutes.

Drain the celeriac in a sieve and leave for a few minutes to steam-dry and then reduce to a coarse purée in a food processor. Pour any juices given out by the fish back into the saucepan and reduce to a few tablespoons of buttery emulsion over medium heat, then stir in the anchovy paste, if using. Flake the fish into a large bowl, discarding any bones, and mix in the mashed celeriac and capers. Mix in the cooking liquid, then the egg. Season the mixture to taste. Take heaping tablespoons of the mixture and form into 12 fishcakes, placing each one on top of a slice of bacon, loosely bringing the ends up over the top (bearing in mind the bacon will contract as it cooks. You can prepare the fishcakes to this point up to a day in advance, in which case cover and chill them until required.

Preheat the oven to 425°F. Arrange the fishcakes in a couple of roasting pans with the bacon ends on the bottom, drizzle with a little oil, and bake for 30 minutes, carefully turning them halfway through.
Carbohydrate 3.4g Protein 23.8g

SIMPLY FISHCAKES
You can also pan-fry the fishcakes, leaving off the bacon. In this case shape them as 6 large or 12 small fishcakes and cook in a little **extra virgin olive oil** in a large, nonstick frying pan over medium heat for about 4 minutes on the first side and 2–3 minutes on the second.
Carbohydrate 3.4g Protein 17.7g

WITH ROAST TOMATOES
Arrange 1 lb **cherry** or **small tomatoes on the vine** in a roasting pan so they fit snugly in a single layer. Drizzle with a tablespoon of **vegetable oil** and another of **balsamic vinegar**, and season them with **sea salt** and **black pepper**. Roast for 15 minutes at 425°F, by which time the tomatoes will be soft and the skins will have burst.
Carbohydrate 6g Protein 18.3g

Chile shrimp stir-fry

With no heat to it, Sichuan pepper has little in common with our traditional fiery peppers. Instead, it is an elegant, rust-red little pod scented with mint and lemongrass. First toasted and then ground and combined with salt, it forms a classic seasoning in Sichuan cooking. Crisp deep-fried squid and shrimp are restaurant favorites, though I prefer to pan-fry at home. For those who don't keep a well-stocked Asian pantry, peanut oil provides just the right hint of nuts to take the place of sesame oil.

Serves 2

½ teaspoon Sichuan peppercorns
1 teaspoon sea salt
4 average heads of bok choy, base trimmed
2 tablespoons peanut oil
1 teaspoon sesame oil (optional)
1 red onion, peeled and thinly sliced downward into long strips
1 medium-hot red chile, seeded and cut into long thin strips
a splash of dark soy sauce
10oz raw peeled large shrimp, patted dry
1 large or 2 small scallions, trimmed and cut into 3-inch thin strips

Heat a small frying pan over low heat, add the peppercorns, and gently toast for a couple of minutes until fragrant, stirring now and again. Grind it in a mortar and pestle, then add the salt and combine.

Halve the heads of bok choy where the stalk meets the leaves and thinly slice lengthwise into 3-inch-long strips. Heat a tablespoon of peanut oil, with a teaspoon of sesame oil if you wish, in a large frying pan over high heat. Add the onion and stir-fry for a minute or two until it begins to color at the edges, then add the bok choy and chile and cook for another couple of minutes until they start to wilt. Season with a splash of soy sauce and transfer to a serving plate. Add another tablespoon of oil to the pan and cook the shrimp for a minute or two until pink and firm. Sprinkle with half the salt and pepper mixture, then mix the shrimp into the bok choy. Sprinkle with the scallions and serve with the rest of the salt and pepper for sprinkling if wished.
Carbohydrate 8.6g Protein 29.3g

FRIES

Fries £1
Fish in batter £3.50
Pies £2.50
Mushy peas £1

MASH, FRIES, OR ROAST?

Frequently the comfort we associate with the dishes we have grown up with has as much to do with the potatoes that go with them. It is the pile of buttery mashed potatoes that comes with a slowly braised casserole of beef, the crispy roast potatoes that are *de rigueur* with our roast chicken, and of course french fries with battered fish and tartare sauce, that induce that cathartic state of well-being. So I feel if we can crack this one then we're halfway there.

Letting other vegetables star in place of potatoes is something many chefs have been practicing for years—think of that silky little turnip purée with a medallion of steak and wild mushrooms, or celeriac with a roast game bird. The only drawback is the no-holds-barred on the addition of butter and cream that rather undoes any potential health benefits.

So here I have tried to combine the best low-carb alternatives to potatoes with healthy cooking methods and additions. I have never seen the point of deep fryers in a home kitchen (or deep-fried food), so no surprise that all the fries that follow are roasted, with just one exception of shallow-frying. And the mash, compared to the aforementioned restaurant version, is positively chaste.

MASHED POTATOES

Mash, in its traditional guise, is basically just a purée of potatoes, and we achieve different results depending on their variety and how we go about reducing them to a pulp. If the potatoes have been pressed through a foodmill, then the mash should by rights be sublimely silky, whereas if it's been pounded with a retro masher, it is likely to be laced with alluring little bits of potato.

And the guidelines for alternatives are pretty much the same. There are some vegetables, such as cauliflower, that are perhaps best "mashed" in a food processor to leave them with a slight texture, while a fibrous vegetable like celeriac is most appealing if you reduce it to a purée in a blender.

All mashes, I think, require something in the way of enriching, and in the recipes that follow I have suggested what I feel to be just enough, without going overboard. For instance, sour cream in place of crème fraîche (normally my default), which has a fraction of the fat, in fact about the same as cream, which is basically little more than the top of the milk. A very rich mash is fine every once in a while (like doughnuts, chocolate cake, and croissants), but the idea here is food that you can eat without angst any day of the week you choose.

Also, like any mashed potato, the purées can be flavored at whim. One of my favorite ruses in recent years has been to make a herb purée pesto-style to spoon over the top and loosely fold into the mash to streak it. Make this with olive oil and it looks healthier by the second.

Carrot and rutabaga mash

This is the ideal accompaniment for many of the pies and casseroles in this book. These two vegetables combine beautifully, and a little freshly grated nutmeg enhances their sweetness.

Serves 6

2 lbs carrots, trimmed, peeled, and
    cut into large chunks
2 lbs rutabaga, skin cut off and cut
    into even-sized chunks
4 tablespoons unsalted butter,
    diced, plus a pat to serve
freshly grated nutmeg
sea salt and freshly ground black
    pepper
milk

Bring a large pan of salted water to a boil, add the carrots and rutabaga, and cook for about 20 minutes or until tender, then drain into a sieve and leave for a few minutes for the surface moisture to evaporate. Purée the vegetables in a blender with the butter, plenty of nutmeg, some seasoning, and enough milk to loosen the mixture. Serve with a pat of butter and grinding of black pepper. *Carbohydrate 17.6g Protein 2g*

ROOT VEGETABLE AND GINGER MASH
You can also scent the mash with fresh ginger, in which case blend it with 1 thick slice **fresh ginger**, peeled and coarsely chopped.

Celeriac mash

Celeriac makes one of the most characterful mashes, readily laced with mustard, when it's fabulous with red meat and guinea fowl. The only caveat is the difficulty sometimes of buying it. In much of Europe, celeriac is as ubiquitous as potatoes, onions, or garlic. Remoulade, the salad of grated celeriac dressed with a mustardy mayonnaise, is the French version of coleslaw, and it also makes its appearance as a purée, in *pot au…* pretty much everything, and as fries, too. So its scarcity is purely a cultural division. These days I buy several roots at a time and keep them as a standby.

Serves 6

a splash of vinegar, (white wine or cider)
3 lbs celeriac, skin cut off, and cut into chunks
3 tablespoons salted butter, diced, plus a pat to serve
sea salt and freshly ground black pepper
freshly grated nutmeg
milk

Bring a large pan of water to a boil and acidulate it with a splash of vinegar. Add the celeriac and simmer for 20–30 minutes until tender. Drain in a colander and leave for a few minutes to steam dry.

Purée the celeriac with the butter, some salt, pepper, and nutmeg in a blender, adding enough milk to kickstart the process and achieve a purée. You'll probably need to do this in batches. Transfer to a serving dish, reheating it first if necessary, and drop a pat of butter in the center.
Carbohydrate 6.3g Protein 3.3g

CELERIAC AND MUSTARD MASH
Stir a teaspoon each of **Dijon** and **grainy mustard** into the finished mash.
Carbohydrate 6.4g Protein 3.4g

Brussels sprout and parsley mash

Try out this one on sprout skeptics because, like cauliflower, I think so often it is the texture of this vegetable that some find off-putting. Turned into a luscious green mash with sour cream, flat-leaf parsley, and a few drops of red wine vinegar, and it is unrecognizable.

Serves 6

2 lbs Brussels sprouts, bottoms trimmed and outer leaves removed
2 scant teaspoons red wine vinegar
⅔ cup sour cream
4 tablespoons coarsely chopped flat-leaf parsley
sea salt and freshly ground black pepper
a pat of salted butter, to serve

Bring a large pan of salted water to a boil, add the sprouts, and simmer for 15–20 minutes until tender. Drain them in a colander and leave for a minute or two for any excess water to evaporate. Place them in the bowl of a food processor with the vinegar, sour cream, parsley, and some seasoning, and process to a smooth purée. Transfer the purée to the saucepan, and gently reheat when required. Serve with a pat of butter dropped into the center.
Carbohydrate 7.4g Protein 6.1g

Broccoli mash

The large flowering heads of broccoli have come to look like a poor relation next to sexier long-stemmed varieties. But here it is the old-fashioned type that we are after (incidentally, these heads are also best for making soups).

Serves 6

2 lbs broccoli florets (trimmed weight)
3 tablespoons salted butter, diced
4 tablespoons extra virgin olive oil, plus extra to serve
sea salt and freshly ground black pepper

Bring a large pan of salted water to a boil and simmer the broccoli florets for about 15 minutes until really soft. Drain the broccoli in a colander, shaking it thoroughly, and reduce to a textured purée in a food processor with the butter, olive oil, and some seasoning. Transfer to a serving dish and pour in a little extra oil.
Carbohydrate 2.9g Protein 6.7g

BROCCOLI AND PARSLEY MASH
Process the broccoli with ½ cup **flat-leaf parsley** to coarsely chop it for a really lively, vibrant mash, and sprinkle with a little extra chopped when serving.

Cauliflower mash

Cauliflower has a delicacy and elegance that comes to the fore when it is puréed. I think it benefits from a slight rusticity of texture, but you can also make a smooth purée by using a blender with enough milk to achieve the right consistency; this makes a *soignée* base for all kinds of delicate fish, some grilled lamb chops, or a rare steak.

Serves 6

2 lbs cauliflower florets (about 2 cauliflowers)
⅔ cup sour cream
sea salt and freshly ground black pepper
freshly grated nutmeg
pat of salted butter, to serve

Bring a large pan of salted water to a boil, add the cauliflower and cook for about 15 minutes until tender. Drain in a colander, leave for a few minutes to steam dry, then blend to a purée in a food processor with the sour cream, some seasoning, and nutmeg. You may need to do this in batches. This can be made in advance and gently reheated. Transfer to a serving dish, grate on a little more nutmeg, and drop a pat of butter in the center.
Carbohydrate 6.2g Protein 6.8g

CAULIFLOWER AND PESTO MASH
Make the purée as above with ½ cup **sour cream** and omit the nutmeg. Process ½ cup **basil leaves**, 3 tablespoons **extra virgin olive oil**, a squeeze of **lemon juice**, and a little **sea salt** to a textured purée in a food processor. Transfer the mash to a serving dish, spoon the purée on top, and fold over a few times until streaked with green. You can also scatter over a few more tiny basil leaves.
Carbohydrate 12g Protein 13.4g

ABOVE: *Roast pumpkin and tomato mash*

Two pumpkin mashes

My local grocer stocks big, French buff-colored pumpkins with a really dark orange aromatic flesh (the variety remains a mystery), and they do make a fabulous mash. Try for one of the heirloom varieties, or ones that are grown with the table in mind rather than those intended to be carved into Halloween horrors, which have only a thin layer of flesh.

ROAST PUMPKIN AND TOMATO MASH

Roasting any vegetable will concentrate its flavor as the juices are driven off and sugars caramelize, and given that pumpkin can be on the tame side, it's an ideal way of cooking it. This particular mash is sharpened with tomatoes and roast garlic, so it goes hand in hand with other Mediterranean flavors.

Serves 6

2 lbs pumpkin flesh (about 3 lbs whole), cut into chunks
3 small tomatoes
4 garlic cloves, unpeeled
extra virgin olive oil
sea salt and freshly ground black pepper
finely chopped flat-leaf parsley, to serve

Preheat the oven to 425°F. Arrange the pumpkin, tomatoes, and garlic in a roasting pan. Drizzle with 4 tablespoons of oil and season. Roast for 50 minutes, until softened and starting to color. Leave for about 10 minutes to cool a little, then slip the skins off the tomatoes (you can wear rubber gloves for this), and squeeze out the insides of the garlic. Purée the contents of the roasting dish in a food processor. Taste for seasoning and reheat if necessary, though it is still good warm. Serve drizzled with oil and sprinkled with parsley.
Carbohydrate 5.7g Protein 1.7g

PUMPKIN AND APPLE MASH

This wintery pumpkin and apple mash is a natural with any meaty sausages. Look out for French sausages such as Toulouse: if they are the genuine article they shouldn't contain any bread. Merguez, typically North African sausages, are also worth researching.

Serves 4

3 tablespoons unsalted butter
2⅔ lbs pumpkin flesh (about 4 lbs whole), coarsely diced
3 apples, peeled, cored, and coarsely diced
¼ cup orange juice
sea salt and freshly ground black pepper
2 tablespoons extra virgin olive oil
a generous squeeze of lemon juice
4 tablespoons snipped chives

Melt the butter in a large saucepan over medium heat and cook the pumpkin and apple for about 5 minutes, stirring frequently. Add the orange juice and plenty of seasoning, cover, and cook over low heat for 15 minutes. Drain off the liquid, and coarsely mash the pumpkin and apple using a potato masher, then stir in the olive oil, a squeeze of lemon juice, and the chives, and taste for seasoning.
Carbohydrate 18.1g Protein 2.8g

Spring root mash

Each of these spring roots provides a different texture, the end result is a delicious mélange of the best of the vegetable patch at that time of year.

Serves 6

3 tablespoons unsalted butter, plus
    a pat to serve
sea salt and freshly ground black
    pepper
14oz small turnips, trimmed,
    peeled, and halved if necessary
3 cups slim carrots, trimmed,
    peeled, and thickly sliced
    diagonally
4 cups slim leeks, thickly sliced
    diagonally
1 tablespoon extra virgin olive oil
freshly grated nutmeg
finely chopped chives, to serve

Bring 2½ cups water to a boil with the butter and a teaspoon of salt in a medium-large saucepan. Add the turnips and carrots, bring the liquid back to a boil, cover, and cook over medium-low heat for 8 minutes, stirring in the leeks after 2 minutes.

Drain and process the contents to a purée in a food processor with the olive oil and a grating of nutmeg, then season to taste. Transfer to a serving dish, drop in a pat of butter, and sprinkle with chives.

FRENCH FRIES

I confess I've never been very big on french fries. I adore the skinny fries that we get in France, but I can pass on most others. As for frozen oven-cooked french fries, why, when there are so many other wonderful alternative vegetable options, go for second best? So the recipes that follow are in my eyes an improvement, even though they are altogether different, and I realize I may have some difficulty convincing the diehards out there to switch camps.

I am inclined to think that a large part of what we love about fries is their shape and the sensation of eating them. I also prize that light crunch of fine sea salt crystals scrunched over at the end, and we can still have that. We can also have the fish, the burgers, and the sausages we love to eat with them. And the ketchup and tartare sauce.

Chunky celeriac fries

These are particularly good with beef, as are rutabaga fries, a vegetable that is horribly overlooked, though I do realize it is not to everyone's taste, while celeriac has more universal appeal.

Serves 4

3½ lbs celeriac, skin cut off and
    sliced into wedges 1 inch thick
7 tablespoons unsalted butter
sea salt
paprika or piment
    d'espelette (optional)

Preheat the oven to 425°F. Arrange the celeriac in a large roasting pan that will hold it in a crowded single layer. Clarify the butter by gently melting it in a small saucepan, skim off the surface foam, and pour the clear liquid over the celeriac, season with salt, and toss to coat it. Roast for 1–1¼ hours, turning with a spatula halfway through. Season with a little paprika or piment d'espelette if wished.
Carbohydrate 8.6g Protein 4.6g

Zucchini fries

We have a local burger place that keeps every member of the family happy, with triple-topped burgers and milkshakes for teenagers, and skinny burgers (i.e., without a bun), and zucchini fries for the likes of myself.

Serves 4

1 large egg
1 tablespoon extra virgin olive oil
sea salt
paprika
4 medium zucchini, ends trimmed, and cut into fries ½ inch diameter and 2–3 inches long

Whisk the egg with the olive oil, 1 tablespoon of still or sparkling water, some salt, and paprika in a large bowl. Toss the zucchini fries with the egg mixture to very lightly coat them. On removing them from the bowl, use a slotted utensil so that any excess egg mixture is left behind.

OVEN-ROASTED
Before dipping the zucchini, preheat the oven to 475°F and use a pastry brush to lightly coat the bottom of a couple of roasting pans with a thin film of olive oil. Spread out the dipped fries in a single layer, and roast for 25–30 minutes until golden, turning them with a spatula halfway through. A lower pan will probably take longer than one on top.
Carbohydrate 3.7g Protein 5.2g

FRIED
Heat about ½ inch of **vegetable oil** in a large frying pan over medium heat until a drop of the egg mixture sizzles when added. Cook the fries in batches for a few minutes, turning them halfway, until golden and crispy. Remove with a slotted spoon and drain on paper towels; stack in a bowl, scrunching on some sea salt.
Carbohydrate 3.7g Protein 5.2g

Thick-cut pumpkin fries

I adore these pumpkin fries. Roasting does them a huge favor and they turn deliciously caramelized.

Serves 4

1⅓ lbs pumpkin flesh, (about 2 lbs whole)
2 tablespoons extra virgin olive oil, plus extra for oiling
2 tablespoons fresh thyme leaves, preferably lemon thyme
sea salt

Preheat the oven to 425°F. Cut the pumpkin into chunky fries roughly an inch in diameter and toss in a large bowl with the olive oil and thyme. Brush the base of a large roasting pan with oil and spread the fries out in a crowded single layer. Roast for 40–45 minutes, carefully turning them halfway through using a spatula. Scrunch on some sea salt, and carefully turn to season them on the other side, then transfer to a bowl to serve.
Carbohydrate 3.7g Protein 1.1g

ROAST

Roasted and grilled vegetables have a luxurious quality when cooked with olive oil. And they will take the place of starchier offerings like potatoes and parsnips when you are after a traditional side.

Roast peppers

These are particularly good once the barbecue season is upon us.

Serves 6

6 red or orange peppers, core,
    seeds, and membranes removed
8–10 fresh thyme sprigs
2 bay leaves
5 garlic cloves, peeled and sliced
4 tablespoons extra virgin olive oil
sea salt and freshly ground black
    pepper
1 teaspoon balsamic vinegar

Preheat the oven to 400°F. Quarter the peppers and arrange in a crowded single layer in a baking dish or roasting pan. Tuck in the herbs and sprinkle with the garlic. Drizzle on the oil and season with salt and pepper.

Roast for 45–50 minutes, stirring and basting at least twice to ensure the peppers emerge succulent and evenly singed at the edges. Remove from the oven, drizzle the vinegar over, and vaguely stir to mix it into the juices. Leave to cool.
Carbohydrate 10.5g Protein 1.8g

Dish up with a selection of hors d'oeuvres—**green** and **black olives**, **salami**, **cornichons**, and **caper berries**.
Carbohydrate 10.7g Protein 3.7g

Crispy roast onions

An alternative to fried onion rings—healthier and easier to cook.

Serves 6

2 lbs red onions, peeled, halved,
    and sliced
extra virgin olive or vegetable oil
1 teaspoon red wine vinegar
sea salt

Preheat the oven to 375°F. Spread out the onions in a thin layer on two baking sheets, breaking the slices into rings as far as possible. Drizzle on a little oil and roast for 35 minutes, stirring halfway through to ensure they caramelize evenly. Remove from the oven, transfer to a bowl, and toss with a teaspoon of vinegar and some salt. Serve warm or at room temperature.
Carbohydrate 12g Protein 1.8g

Chargrilled zucchini

Another great basic that you can cook well in advance, which makes for relaxed grazing with all the usual Mediterranean goodies like sun-dried tomatoes, olives, and prosciutto. And you can also build them into a salad, or serve them very simply with some roast chicken or chops.

Serves 6

4 zucchini, ends removed,
  cut into long thin strips
extra virgin olive oil
sea salt and freshly ground black
  pepper

Heat a ridged cast-iron grill pan over medium-high heat, brush one side of as many zucchini slices as will fit with olive oil, season and grill this side for 3–5 minutes until striped with gold, then brush the top side, turn and grill this side, too. Transfer them to a plate and grill the remainder in the same fashion, then leave the slices to cool. You can cook them well in advance.
Carbohydrate 3.5g Protein 2.3g

AS A SALAD WITH OLIVES
Shortly before eating, scatter 3 **scallions**, trimmed and thinly sliced diagonally, and 1 cup pitted **black olives** over the zucchini, drizzle with a little more oil, and dust with **paprika**.
Carbohydrate 3.7g Protein 2.5g

Roast carrot wedges

This turns a humble root into a star of a dish. Good with a roast, or you can leave them to cool a little and toss them into a pile of salad leaves with some crispy bacon or ham. You want good-sized roots, not real brutes, but not tiny ones either—they will only shrivel up on cooking.

Serves 6

4 tablespoons extra virgin olive oil
2 lbs chunky carrots, peeled, halved
  lengthwise, and halved into
  2 shorter lengths
1 large onion, peeled and cut into
  thin wedges
several bay leaves
1 head of garlic, broken into cloves
sea salt and freshly ground black
  pepper

Preheat the oven to 425°F. Heat 2 tablespoons of olive oil over high heat in a large heavy-duty roasting dish (about 10 × 15 inches) on the stovetop. Add the carrots and cook for about 10 minutes, stirring frequently, until well on the way to being colored, adding the onion halfway through. This gives the veggies a head start before their roasting. Now toss in the bay leaves and garlic, season generously, drizzle with another couple of tablespoons of oil, and roast for 40–50 minutes until golden on the outside and soft within, stirring halfway through. The insides of the garlic cloves can be squeezed out and eaten.
Carbohydrate 17.1g Protein 1.9g

Grilled eggplant

These thick slices are delicately caramelized on the outside and meltingly creamy within. Endlessly versatile, you can eat them with anything and everything.

Serves 6

3 eggplants, ends discarded, cut into 1 inch slices
extra virgin olive oil
sea salt and freshly ground black pepper

Preheat the oven to 425°F. Lay the eggplant out on a couple of baking sheets, brushing the slices with oil on both sides and seasoning the top. Roast for 20 minutes, then turn them and cook for another 10–20 minutes until golden; the lower baking sheet may need longer than the top. Loosen with a spatula and serve hot or cold.
Carbohydrate 3.5g Protein 1.4g

AS A SALAD
Lay the slices out on a large platter, top each one with a spoonful of **Greek yogurt**, and sprinkle with **pomegranate seeds** and coarsely chopped **cilantro** or **flat-leaf parsley**.
Carbohydrate 6.9g Protein 4.1g

Roasted roots

This offers a gorgeous blast of color and flavor, great with any roast, including fish. And, like most roast vegetables, they are good for snacking on at room temperature.

Serves 4

14oz celeriac, skin cut off and sliced into wedges ½ inch thick
14oz beets, tops and tails trimmed, cut into wedges
6 medium carrots, halved lengthwise and cut into two shorter lengths
5 tablespoons unsalted butter
sea salt and freshly ground black pepper

Preheat the oven to 425°F. Arrange the vegetables in a large roasting pan that will hold them in a crowded single layer. Clarify the butter by gently melting it in a small saucepan, skim off the surface foam, and pour the clear liquid over the vegetables, discarding the milky solids below. Season with salt and pepper and toss to coat. Roast for 70–75 minutes until golden, turning with a spatula halfway through.
Carbohydrate 18.5g Protein 3.9g

WITH PERSILLADE
Sprinkle the roast vegetables with persillade, and serve them with air-dried ham and olives.

Make a persillade by whizzing ⅓ cup **flat-leaf parsley** and 2 peeled **garlic cloves** in a food processor until very finely chopped. Sprinkle over the vegetables and serve.
Carbohydrate 19.5g Protein 10.4g

ABOVE: *Roasted roots (see page 169)*

ABOVE: *Roasted roots with Persillade (see page 169)*

OTHER LOVELY VEGGIES

This is a mélange of vegetable dishes that don't quite fit "mash, fries, or roast," or salad, but look beyond steamed or lightly blanched. And there is nothing wrong with either of those ways of preparation, especially if there is a sauce or some juice to dress them. But we start with a few dishes, cooked with a minimum of fuss—broccoli for instance, which can be grilled, smothered, or sautéed, and cabbages in endless guises. We might not want them in Miracle Soups but I grow even fonder of these vegetables with every year that passes.

There are a handful of stand-ins: a rösti, made with root vegetables that are deliciously crispy around the edges; an oven-baked bubble and squeak, where rutabaga stars in the place of potatoes; and the aptly named spaghetti squash. When it's in season, this is about as close as nature gets to providing a plate of noodles. In addition to dressing it with the garlic butter suggested here, the method of cooking it will provide the foundation for any number of other ways you might want to serve it. And, finally, there are a few composite vegetable dishes, ones that will stand on their own, or at least with precious little else.

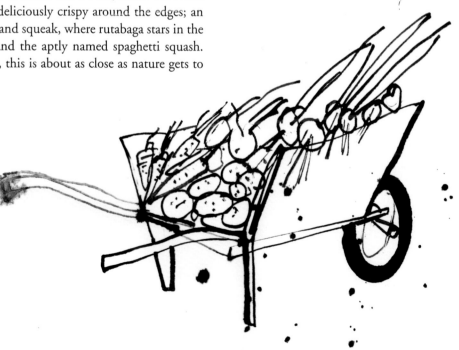

Green beans with smoky bacon

I still regard green beans, or haricots verts, when they are as skinny as a reed and very lightly cooked and tossed with a pat of salty butter, as conceivably the ultimate in vegetable luxury. So it is only one more step to combine them with silky whole shallots and crispy lardons. Serve these with a roast, or equally with an egg, poached or fried, and there is no need to elaborate any more.

Serves 4

2 tablespoons salted butter
½ teaspoon sea salt
8oz small shallots, peeled
5oz smoked bacon, sliced
12oz fine green beans, topped and
    tailed

Heat the butter in a small saucepan with the salt and 2 tablespoons of water until simmering. Add the whole peeled shallots, cover, and cook over low heat for 15 minutes, by which time they should be tender and sitting in a buttery sauce, the water having evaporated.

At the same time heat a large nonstick frying pan over medium heat, add the bacon, and cook for 8–12 minutes until golden and crisp, stirring now and again. Drain the bacon on a double thickness of paper towels and leave to cool. You can prepare the shallots and bacon to this point in advance.

Bring a large pan of salted water to a boil, add the beans, and simmer for 3–5 minutes until just tender. Drain them in a colander and leave for a moment for the surface water to evaporate. Gently reheat the shallots then toss in the hot beans, coating them with the butter, and then the bacon.
Carbohydrate 4.9g Protein 9.8g

Duo of brassicas

Cauliflower is a little like potatoes in that it struggles to find its voice without a supporting cast. So combining it with broccoli, which has a sufficiently different character, creates interest.

Serves 4

4 tablespoons extra virgin olive oil
3 garlic cloves, peeled and thinly
    sliced
½ teaspoon sea salt, preferably
    Maldon
10oz cauliflower florets (1½inches)
10oz broccolini or broccoli, halved
    lengthwise

Put 1⅔ cups water in a medium saucepan with the olive oil, garlic, and salt, and bring to a boil. Add the cauliflower, bring the liquid back to a boil, cover, and cook over medium-low heat for 10 minutes, stirring in the broccoli after 4 minutes, then drain and serve.
Carbohydrate 2.3g Protein 2.7g

Broccoli three ways—grilled/sautéed/steamed

There is less waste with broccolini than the standard sort. They are more like asparagus in that you can eat most of the stalk down to where it becomes visibly tough or pale in color. I particularly like the texture of the heads of broccolini, too. But in a pinch, all these recipes can be prepared with regular broccoli.

Serves 4

14oz broccolini, stems trimmed
extra virgin olive oil
sea salt and freshly ground black
    pepper

GRILLED

Bring a large saucepan of salted water to a boil. Add the broccolini to a boiling water, pushing it well down, and cook for 3 minutes, then drain in a colander and leave for a few minutes to steam-dry.

Heat a grill pan over medium heat. Toss the broccolini in a large bowl with oil to coat it and season. Grill in batches for about 2 minutes on either side until patched with gold. It can be served hot or cold.
Carbohydrate 2.7g Protein 3.3g

Serves 4

4 tablespoons extra virgin olive oil
14oz broccolini, trimmed
sea salt and freshly ground black
    pepper

SAUTÉED

Heat a couple of tablespoons of oil in a large frying pan over medium heat. Add half the broccolini, season, and cook for 3–4 minutes until colored, turning halfway through. Add a generous splash of water to the pan, put on a lid, and cook for about 5 minutes over lowish heat until the thickest parts of the stalks are tender. Transfer this to a plate (you can cover it with foil to keep it warm), and cook the other half in the same way.
Carbohydrate 2.7g Protein 3.3g

Serves 6

2 lbs broccolini, trimmed
3 tablespoons butter
sea salt and freshly ground black
    pepper

STEAMED

Give the broccolini a good rinse in a colander, then place in a large saucepan with 4 tablespoons water, dot with the butter, and season. Cover and cook over medium heat for about 15 minutes until tender, stirring halfway through.
Carbohydrate 3.7g Protein 5.3g

Cavolo nero with anchovies, chile, and garlic

For some years after this vegetable appeared, I was still looking over the shoulders of the fans gathering around it, wondering what all the fuss was about. And then realization dawned— I tried dressing it with olive oil, lemon juice, anchovies, and chile, and cupid's arrow struck.

Serves 4

sea salt
about 1⅓ lbs cavolo nero
5 tablespoons extra virgin olive oil
4 garlic cloves, peeled and finely chopped
1 tablespoon finely chopped medium-hot red chile (seeds discarded)
12 salted anchovy fillets, sliced across
2 tablespoons lemon juice

Bring a large saucepan two-thirds full with salted water to a boil. Cut the cavolo nero leaves off the thin central stalk (even the finest sections at the tip will be tough if left) and then thickly slice the leaves across.

Add the leaves to the pan and cook for 3 minutes, pushing them down now and again so they cook evenly. At the same time, heat a tablespoon of oil in a nonstick frying pan over medium heat, add the garlic and chile, and cook briefly, stirring frequently, until the garlic is sizzling and just starting to color, then remove from the heat and stir in the anchovies to warm, followed by the lemon juice and another 2 tablespoons of oil.

Drain the cavolo nero in a colander and press out the excess water using the back of a wooden spoon or a potato masher, return to the pan, and toss with a couple of tablespoons of oil. Transfer this to a serving plate and drizzle with the contents of the frying pan.
Carbohydrate 3g Protein 8.5g

Buttery spring roots

This is the root equivalent of Duo of brassicas (see page 174), and the same goes for combining several different vegetables: they are all the more lavish than served on their own.

Serves 4

2 tablespoons unsalted butter
½ teaspoon sea salt, eg Maldon
½ teaspoon sugar
7oz small turnips, trimmed, peeled, and halved if necessary
2 cups slim carrots, trimmed, peeled, and thickly sliced diagonally
2 cups slim leeks, thickly sliced diagonally

Bring 1¼ cups water to a boil with the butter, salt, and sugar in a medium-large saucepan. Add the turnips and carrots, bring the liquid back to a boil, cover, and cook over medium-low heat for 8 minutes, stirring in the leeks after 2 minutes, then drain off the liquid.
Carbohydrate 7.1g Protein 1.6g

Crispy cabbage gratin

Of the many vegetables of which I am the sole member of the Appreciation Society (within my own family), none is met with greater disdain than Brussels sprouts. I adore sprouts, but for the most part we all save them for a once-a-year Christmas blow-out, and even then curse them for the time they take to trim and the fact they exist at all.

Sprouts have a sophisticated edge, and it's easy enough to see why children might not take to the curious bitterness that defines them, but I would put them in the same league as blue cheese and Angostura Bitters as a taste worth acquiring.

If there is any justification for hating them, then surely it has to do with their being boiled. Two ways around this are to cook and purée, or sauté them, especially with a bit of bacon. But it was revelation to discover one idle suppertime that they actually roast a treat, too. So if you happen to be one of those doubters, give this one a try.

Serves 6

1–1½ white or green cabbage, base trimmed, outer leaves discarded
1 lb Brussels sprouts, base trimmed, outer leaves discarded and halved downward
1 red onion, peeled, halved, and thinly sliced
4 tablespoons extra virgin olive oil
sea salt and freshly ground black pepper

Preheat the oven to 425°F. Cut the cabbage into thin wedges, leaving them attached by the thick central stalk at the base, then cut in half any sections longer than about 4 inches. Arrange the cabbage, sprouts, and the red onion in a large roasting pan (about 10 × 15 inches), drizzle with the olive oil, season, and toss to coat everything. Roast for about 40 minutes, stirring every 15 minutes, until golden and crispy at the edges.
Carbohydrate 8.9g Protein 4.8g

Savoy cabbage with caraway

There is no accompaniment that suits a slowly roasted cut of meat quite like a big bowl of cabbage. And of all the varieties, Savoy has to be the first choice. Both caraway and chile bring out the best in cabbage, but it's best to exercise a cautious hand—a little of both spices goes a long way.

Serves 4

1 Savoy cabbage, base trimmed, outer leaves discarded
⅓ teaspoon caraway seeds
2 tablespoons extra virgin olive oil
a small pinch of red pepper flakes
sea salt

Quarter the cabbage and cut out the core, then finely slice the leaves (since they are so tightly packed, I tend not to bother to wash them). Lightly pound the caraway seeds in a mortar and pestle to break them up. Heat the oil in a large saucepan over medium heat, add the caraway and red pepper flakes and give it a stir, then add the cabbage, season with salt, and stir-fry for a couple of minutes until it is glossy. Add 3 tablespoons of water, put on a lid, and cook over low heat for 15 minutes, or until the toughest parts are tender, stirring halfway through. The cabbage is quite good-natured and can be reheated if wished. Any leftover makes a delicious bubble and squeak (see page 182).
Carbohydrate 8g Protein 4.3g

WHITE CABBAGE WITH NUTMEG

Discarding any damaged outer leaves, quarter a **white cabbage**, cut out the core and slice wafer-fine into strands 2–3 inches long. Melt 2 tablespoons **unsalted butter** in a large saucepan over medium-low heat, add the cabbage, season with **sea salt**, **freshly ground black pepper,** and a generous grating of **nutmeg,** and cook for 5–10 minutes, stirring frequently, until relaxed and lightly colored.
Carbohydrate 7.9g Protein 2.2g

Swiss chard with cilantro, allspice, and pomegranate

Like so many cabbages, Swiss chard greets spices and fruits like old friends—they go very well together, and any potential austerity is further softened by a mass of golden fried onions and a generous addition of cilantro.

Serves 6

3 tablespoons extra virgin olive oil
2 large onions, peeled, halved, and finely sliced across
a splash of vinegar (white wine or cider)
1¼ lbs Swiss chard
½ teaspoon allspice
sea salt
½ cup coarsely chopped cilantro
sumac (optional)
3 heaping tablespoons pomegranate seeds

Heat 2 tablespoons of oil in a large saucepan over medium heat and cook the onions for 15–20 minutes, stirring frequently, until creamy and golden.

At the same time, bring a large saucepan of water to a boil and acidulate it with a splash of vinegar. Cut the chard leaves off the stalks and thickly slice them, then thinly slice the stalks. Add the stalks to the pan and cook for 5 minutes, then add the leaves and cook for another 2 minutes. Drain in a colander and shake dry.

Stir the allspice into the onions, and then add the chard. Season with salt and gently cook for a couple of minutes to acquaint the ingredients, then stir in the cilantro. Transfer to a serving dish, drizzle with the remaining tablespoon of oil, sprinkle on some sumac if wished and then the pomegranate seeds.
Carbohydrate 9.6g Protein 2.6g

Oven-baked bubble and squeak

This bubble and squeak, cooked in the oven, is easier than hovering over a frying pan. Although it is also a bit heartier than the stovetop version, it works well as a side dish for any of the casseroles, or on its own with poached or fried eggs, broiled tomatoes, and mushrooms. And crispy bacon.

Serves 6

3⅓ lbs rutabaga, skin cut off and
    cut into even-sized chunks
2 tablespoons vegetable oil
3 tablespoons unsalted butter
1 onion, peeled and finely chopped
3½ cups coarsely chopped Savoy
    cabbage
sea salt and freshly ground black
    pepper
1 heaping teaspoon grainy mustard
a couple of handfuls of coarsely
    chopped flat-leaf parsley

Bring a large saucepan of salted water to a boil, add the rutabaga, and cook for 20–30 minutes until tender, then drain in a colander, return to the pan, and coarsely mash using a potato masher. Press out the excess liquid from the rutabaga in a sieve in batches, again using a potato masher, and transfer to a large bowl.

Heat a tablespoon of oil and half the butter in a large frying pan over medium heat, add the onion, and cook for a few minutes, stirring occasionally, until glossy and starting to color, then add the cabbage and cook for a couple of minutes longer, turning constantly, until it relaxes. Combine the onion and cabbage with the rutabaga, season generously, and stir in the mustard and the parsley. You can prepare the dish to this point in advance, in which case leave to cool, cover, and chill.

Preheat the oven to 425°F. Drizzle a tablespoon of oil over the base of a cast-iron or other roasting dish (about 8 × 12 inches) and place in the oven for 10 minutes. Press the rutabaga mixture into the hot pan, leaving the surface on the rough side. Dot with the remaining butter and bake for 35–40 minutes until golden at the tips and around the edge.
Carbohydrate 15.8g Protein 3g

Spaghetti squash with garlic butter

I recall being surprised, charmed and amazed the very first time I cut a spaghetti squash open and forked its flesh into fine strands, hence the name. They merit any pasta or noodle-like treatment, here slightly decadently with garlic butter and Parmesan, but add this to your personal taste.

Serves 4

Spaghetti squash:
1 × 4 lb spaghetti squash
freshly grated Parmesan to serve
  (optional)

Garlic butter:
7 tablespoons unsalted butter,
  softened
2 garlic cloves, peeled and coarsely
  chopped
zest of 1 lemon, plus a generous
  squeeze of juice
sea salt and freshly ground black
  pepper
3 tablespoons finely chopped
  flat-leaf parsley
2 tablespoons finely chopped chives

If you don't have a pot large enough to hold the entire spaghetti squash, simply cut off the stalk end to fit. Half-fill the pan with water and bring to a boil. Prick the squash all over with a skewer. Add to the pan, cover, and simmer over low heat for 40 minutes or until tender when pierced with a knife, turning it over halfway through.

In the meantime place the butter, garlic, lemon zest and juice, and some seasoning in the bowl of a food processor and blend at high speed until creamy and amalgamated. Add the chopped herbs and give another pulse to incorporate them. This can also be made well in advance.

Remove the squash from the pan, slice in half lengthwise, and scoop out the seeds, then fork the flesh into a large bowl into long spaghetti strands. Transfer this into a sieve, set it back over the bowl, and press out the excess liquid using a potato masher. Transfer the spaghetti strands to a shallow serving dish and fork to separate the lump a little. Half melt the garlic butter in a small saucepan and pour this over, cutting through the squash a few times to roughly mix it in. Serve with freshly grated Parmesan if wished.
Carbohydrate 16.3g Protein 2.5g

Baked leeks, endive, and prosciutto

Both leeks and endive turn delectably succulent when braised. One is sweet, the other slightly bitter, and the prosciutto salty—a perfect storm. As well as being delicious on its own, this will lend its hand as a side to roast chicken, or for eating cold with a sheep cheese.

Serves 4

1¼ lbs leeks, halved lengthwise
3 garlic cloves, peeled and cut into
    2–3 slivers
1 cup white wine
6 tablespoons extra virgin olive oil
1 tablespoon soft thyme leaves
sea salt and freshly ground black
    pepper
4 heads of endive, base trimmed,
    outer leaves discarded, and halved
    lengthwise
1 tablespoon white wine vinegar
8 slices prosciutto
coarsely chopped flat-leaf parsley
    (optional)

Preheat the oven to 350°F. Arrange the leeks, cut side up, lengthwise in a crowded single layer in a suitable roasting pan (about 8 × 12 inches), overlapping as necessary and tucking the garlic in between. Pour in the wine and drizzle with 3 tablespoons of oil. Sprinkle on the thyme and season. Toss the endive with a couple of tablespoons of oil and the vinegar in a large bowl and arrange, cut side down, on top of the leeks, so they lie lengthwise in the same fashion, and season them. Cover with foil and bake for 1 hour.

Turn up the oven temperature to 425°F. Uncover the roasting pan, baste the vegetables with the juices, then drape a slice of prosciutto along each half of endive (this will shrink as it cooks). Drizzle on another tablespoon of oil and return to the oven for 20 minutes or until the prosciutto is golden and crisp. Serve hot or at room temperature with the juices drizzled on, sprinkled with parsley if wished.

Carbohydrate 9.6g Protein 9.4g

Root vegetable and apple gratin

This will take the place of potatoes with roast pork or lamb, and you can also use rutabaga in place of celeriac. Try to slice the vegetables as thinly as possible to avoid gaps when you layer them, a task that is best done by hand.

Serves 6

1⅓ lbs celeriac, skin cut off, cut downward into wedges and finely sliced

5 cups carrots, trimmed, peeled, and finely sliced

4 tablespoons extra virgin olive oil

2 garlic cloves, peeled and finely chopped

2 teaspoons finely chopped fresh rosemary, plus a few needles

sea salt and freshly ground black pepper

2 red-skinned apples, quartered, cored, and thinly sliced lengthwise

Preheat the oven to 400°F. Toss the celeriac and carrots separately in large bowls with 3 tablespoons of olive oil (1½ tablespoons in each), the garlic, chopped rosemary, and some seasoning. Arrange the celeriac in a layer in a gratin or shallow ovenproof dish (about 8 × 12 inches), with the carrot on top, cover tightly with foil, and bake for 50 minutes until the vegetables are tender when pierced with a knife.

Distribute the apple over the surface with a few rosemary needles, drizzle with another tablespoon of oil and return to the oven for 15 minutes, then pop under the broiler to color the top.
Carbohydrate 15.5g Protein 2.1g

Sautéed mixed mushrooms

There is no rocket science to this recipe—if anything it is here as a reminder. I find if I am cooking something in season and there has been a gap of many months since the last time, I may have forgotten the way I felt was "best," and need to look back at past notes and recipes.

Serves 4

4 tablespoons olive oil
2 shallots, peeled and finely chopped
1 garlic clove, peeled and finely chopped (optional)
1 lb mixture wild and cultivated mushrooms, picked over and sliced as necessary
sea salt and freshly ground black pepper
a squeeze of lemon juice
2 heaping tablespoons finely chopped flat-leaf parsley

Cook the mushrooms in two batches. Heat half the oil in a large frying pan over medium heat, add half the shallots, and cook for a moment until they soften. Add half the garlic (if including) and half the mushrooms, turn up the heat, and toss constantly until they are soft and starting to color, seasoning them toward the end. If any liquid is given out in the process, keep cooking until it evaporates. Transfer the mushrooms to a bowl and cook the remainder likewise.

Return all the mushrooms to the pan, season with a squeeze of lemon juice, and stir in the parsley.
Carbohydrate 2.5g Protein 2.4g

Tapas-style mushrooms

Eggs any which way come to mind as an accompaniment here, scrambled, poached, or fried, in time for brunch, but then again, they make wonderful nibbles with an apéritif of a small glass of dry fino.

Serves 6

3 tablespoons extra virgin olive oil
4 shallots, peeled, halved, and sliced
10 thin slices of chorizo, cut into thin strips
1 lb brown and button mushrooms, trimmed, and halved if large
sea salt and freshly ground black pepper
½ cup Madeira or medium sherry
coarsely chopped cilantro leaves

Heat 2 tablespoons of the olive oil in a large frying pan over medium-high heat, add the shallots and chorizo, and cook for 4–7 minutes until lightly golden, stirring occasionally. Add the mushrooms and another tablespoon of oil, season, and cook for about 5 minutes longer, until the onions are a deep gold and the mushrooms lightly colored.

Pour in the Madeira and simmer for a few minutes until the juices are really rich and dark. You can also cook these in advance and briefly reheat them.

Serve right away scattered with cilantro.
Carbohydrate 2g Protein 3.4g

Root vegetable rösti

Any vegetable that is grated and then fried is going to make deliciously delicate and crispy wisps, and these rösti are no exception. Ham? A tempting marriage, given the sweetness of the roots. If any leftover shreds are going begging, all the better, but otherwise some pulled or shredded ham hock will play the part.

Serves 4

4 carrots, trimmed and peeled
9oz rutabaga, skin cut off
1 small onion, peeled
2 large eggs
1 teaspoon grainy mustard
sea salt and freshly ground black
  pepper
1 cup shredded or diced ham
  (optional)
vegetable oil for frying

Bring a large saucepan of salted water to a boil. Coarsely grate and combine the carrots, rutabaga, and onion—the quickest route here is a food processor using the coarse grating attachment, picking out any chunky slivers. Add the grated vegetables to the boiling water and blanch for 2 minutes, then drain in a sieve and press out as much liquid as possible using a potato masher. Transfer the grated vegetables to a large bowl and leave to cool to room temperature. You can prepare it to this point an hour or two in advance, in which case cover and set aside.

Whisk the eggs with the mustard, mix this into the vegetables, and season the mixture. Fold in the ham if wished. Heat a tablespoon of oil in a large, nonstick frying pan over medium heat, and drop heaping tablespoons of the mixture into the pan, gently but firmly pressing each mound down with a spatula to form a patty about ½ inch thick with ragged edges. You will probably be able to fit about 3 in the pan at a time. Cook for 2–3 minutes until the underside is golden and crispy, then carefully turn, using a spatula because they are quite delicate, and cook for a couple of minutes longer. Cook the remainder in the same fashion, adding more oil to the pan with each batch or as necessary. You should get 8–9 in all—they can be kept warm in a very low oven if wished.
Carbohydrate 9.6g Protein 4.3g

Mushrooms baked with garlic, lemon, and chile

Simply a delicious way of cooking any kind of flat-cap mushrooms, using their gently concave cups to hold the juices given out as they bake, and mingle with the jazzy trio of garlic, chile, and lemon. Like any mushroom, these are the perfect side to roast or grilled meat, or with bacon and fried eggs.

Serves 4

8 medium flat mushrooms
4 garlic cloves, peeled and finely
    chopped
1 medium-hot red chile, core and
    seeds removed and finely chopped
finely grated zest of 1 lemon, plus
    1 tablespoon of juice
3 tablespoons extra virgin olive oil
2 tablespoons unsalted butter
sea salt and freshly ground black
    pepper
2 tablespoons coarsely chopped
    flat-leaf parsley

Preheat the oven to 400°F. Trim the ends of the mushroom stems and arrange them in a baking dish cup-side up. Divide the garlic, chile, and lemon zest among the cups. Drizzle with the olive oil, dot with the butter, season, and bake for 25 minutes.

Remove from the oven, sprinkle the lemon juice over the mushrooms, and then the parsley. Serve hot or warm.
Carbohydrate 1.6g Protein 2.7g

THE SALAD COUNTER

There is no point in pretending that bread and lettuce leaves have anything in common, but for as long as I can remember I have been using crisp green leaves to the same advantage that others do rolls. It started as a preference over crackers to go with cheese—I found a salty sliver of Comté or gooey river of Vacherin altogether more appealing when slipped on top of a small leaf, especially when there were walnuts to crack. Then it moved on to dipping slightly bitter leaves of Belgian endive into taramasalata and guacamole or whatever I was grazing on, as opposed to a piece of pita. While others would eat smoked salmon on a slice of buttered brown bread, my choice again was a leaf of lettuce.

So throughout this book, whenever I repeat my mantra of "lettuce, lettuce, lettuce," please understand it is heartfelt, not something I am suggesting is a good idea simply in the name of reducing carbs. I would far sooner pair rich offerings with the clean austerity of salad than with the starchy dryness of a loaf.

So much of the way we eat is to do with conditioning and habit. Snacking on bread and toast is engrained into us from the earliest age, by busy moms for whom it represents the simplest home-cooked offering. If the bread is good and likewise what you put on it, surely that is better than a processed hot dog, or so the thinking goes. And then as we get older, probably as our first stab at independent living, most parents will suggest to their children making themselves some toast as an elementary exploration into cooking. Come college, if there is a communal kitchen, the likelihood is the provision will run to bread, butter, jam and the like, and a variety of beverages.

But it is possible to change the way you eat. In France, men of a certain age often sport what might politely be coined "baguette belly." The more traditional French, in areas where a two-hour lunchbreak is still the norm, will travel home at lunchtime, or perhaps go to a local restaurant where they will eat their main meal of the day. The two or three courses it entails are usually fairly healthy. Some salads to begin, then an entrée of meat and one or two veg, a sliver or two of cheese. But, it is quite usual for the diner to consume up to half a long baguette. Supper is likely to be a smaller meal, some *soupe* perhaps and a piece of fruit. But again the soup is consumed with another half baguette.

One of our neighbors in Normandy with a "baguette belly" decided he wanted to lose it. So, he gave up his beloved loaf, which must have taken an iron will because I recall him refusing even to sit down to a meal if it was absent, and over the period of a year the weight simply dropped off. That was the only change that he made in his diet. Frequently, I believe, it can be just one small change that is the difference between slowly putting on weight until you enter the rollercoaster ride of yo-yo dieting, and maintaining a healthy weight with which you are happy. If you habitually snack on bread, it could be that toning this down is all you need to do in order to stop gaining. So, lettuce leaf or bread?

Hot five dressings

GREEN GODDESS

This is much more than a dressing, voluptuously silken and creamy, and like a mayonnaise, you could slather it onto pretty much anything with assured results. It is likely to be a little more than you will need for the salad, but as well as *crudités*, you could stir some cooked diced green vegetables and capers into it.

Serves 8

2 large eggs
⅔ cup extra virgin olive oil
2 tablespoons lemon juice
½ garlic clove, chopped
⅓ cup flat-leaf parsley
sea salt and freshly ground black
  pepper

Bring a small saucepan of water to a boil and cook the eggs for 1 minute, then drain the pan, refill with cold water, and leave them to cool for a couple of minutes. Scoop the insides of the eggs into a blender, including the thin layer of cooked white lining the shell, and blend with all the remaining dressing ingredients to a creamy green emulsion. Cover and chill until required. The dressing will keep well for a couple of days.
Carbohydrate 0.3g Protein 1.7g

Serves 8

2 small heads Belgian endive
2 cups watercress sprigs
2 cups pea shoots
2 avocados, quartered and pitted
1 container of sprouts, such as
  mustard and cress, cut
⅓ cup pitted or stuffed green
  olives, halved
1 tablespoon snipped chives

SERVING SUGGESTION

Trim the base of the heads of the endive, discard any damaged outer leaves, then cut in half lengthwise and thinly slice, and halve again into shorter lengths. Combine these on a serving dish with the watercress and pea shoots. Peel the skin off the avocado quarters and cut into long thin strips.

Drizzle some of the dressing over the leaves, distribute the avocado, and drizzle over a little more dressing, then dot with clumps of mustard and cress, finally adding the olives and some chives.
Carbohydrate 1.3g Protein 3.4g

REAL FRENCH DRESSING

I love this particular dressing for its honest, flinty, down-to-earth profile. Sometimes we talk of vegetable oils as being neutral or tasteless, but they all have their own savor, however subtle. I prefer peanut (or arachide) to sunflower oil, and I also find it tends to emulsify better, so unless you are avoiding peanuts this will give the best results.

Serves 6

1 rounded teaspoon Dijon mustard
sea salt and freshly ground black
  pepper
3 tablespoons peanut oil
1 teaspoon vinegar (red wine or cider)

Whisk the mustard with a little seasoning in a medium bowl, scrunching the salt if it is flaky. Whisk in the oil a tablespoon at a time, until thick and mayonnaise-like. Stir in the vinegar and then about 2 teaspoons of water to thin the vinaigrette to the consistency of cream.
Carbohydrate 0.3g Protein 0.1g

ANCHOVY AND LEMON

One of the best dressings for endive, be it Belgian or the leafier types.

Serves 4

**finely grated zest of 1 lemon, plus
2 tablespoons juice**
**6 salted anchovy fillets, finely
chopped**
**1 teaspoon finely chopped
medium-hot red chile**
sea salt
½ cup extra virgin olive oil

Whisk together the lemon zest and juice, anchovies, chile, and a little salt in a medium bowl, then whisk in the oil.

Carbohydrate 0.2g Protein 1.6g

SERVING SUGGESTION

Endive gives out lots of liquid once it's dressed, especially in the company of anchovies, so toss it as close to eating as possible.

Serves 4

**8 heads of Belgian endive, ideally
red**
**a handful of coarsely chopped
flat-leaf parsley**

Trim the base of the heads of endive, discard any damaged outer leaves, then cut in half lengthwise and thinly slice into long thin strips. Transfer to a salad bowl, pour in the dressing and toss, then mix in some parsley.

Carbohydrate 8.3g Protein 3g

CAESAR

In a true Caesar salad, the dressing is only half the story, with Parmesan sharing the stage. But actually it's a great dressing in its own right, and I frequently use it on its own with salads. Its tendency toward bitter/sharp makes it good for slightly sweeter salads, which could be as simple as the addition of some avocado or tomato. It's a good one when you want something with the luxurious quality of a mayonnaise, but which is considerably easier to make.

Serves 8

2 large eggs
½ garlic clove, chopped
2 tablespoons lemon juice
2 teaspoons Worcestershire sauce
⅔ cup extra virgin olive oil
sea salt and freshly ground black
 pepper

Bring a small saucepan of water to a boil and cook the eggs for 1 minute, then drain the pan, refill with cold water, and leave them to cool for a couple of minutes. Scoop the insides of the eggs into a blender, including the thin layer of cooked white lining the shell, and blend with all the remaining dressing ingredients to a pale and creamy emulsion. Cover and chill until required. The dressing will keep well for a couple of days.
Carbohydrate 0.4g Protein 1.6g

SERVING SUGGESTION

This is a basic Caesar salad, but you can build it up in any way you wish, with slivers of avocado and chicken, crispy bacon, other leaves, or finely sliced radishes.

Serves 4

4 Romaine lettuce hearts
¾ cup freshly grated Parmesan

Separate out the lettuce leaves, discarding any outer leathery or blowsy dark green leaves (these can be saved for a soup or purée, or trimmed for slicing into another salad). Arrange the Romaine leaves on two large sharing plates or four dinner plates. Pour over some of the dressing, scatter over the Parmesan and serve immediately.
Carbohydrate 1.8g Protein 8.7g

SOUR CREAM AND MUSTARD

Another rich and voluptuous dressing that is mayonnaise-like in style. This makes a generous quantity; I find it has many uses, but half this amount should do for a family supper. A little sugar to taste is not a bad idea if dressing cabbage, for instance, or leaves that have a bitter edge.

Serves 6

1 cup sour cream
2 teaspoons Dijon mustard
a squeeze of lemon juice
sea salt and freshly ground black
 pepper

Combine all the ingredients in a medium bowl, cover, and chill until required. It will keep well for several days.
Carbohydrate 1.8g Protein 1.2g

Leafy ensembles

Almost any selection of salad leaves that you assemble is going to be streets ahead of a packaged combo: nothing beats leaves that have been carefully picked over by hand and then washed in a sink of very cold water to crisp and restore their just-picked liveliness.

My mother, I remember, always used to wrap the leaves in a towel and give it a good shake outside to dry them, which as far as I could tell seemed to involve transferring the water from your leaves to your clothes. A salad spinner is much easier and assures perfectly dry leaves, without damaging them. It is one piece of equipment worth investing in (see page 14); flimsy spinners or ones with pull strings make my mother's method seem skilled.

Layer **Boston lettuce heart leaves, lamb's quarters, mâche,** or **pea shoots,** and finally **sprouts, like mustard and cress** or **micro greens.**

Combine **lamb's lettuce,** or **mâche,** with **baby ruby chard** or **baby spinach,** and **red or green mustard and cress.** Also lovely with cooked **asparagus spears.**

Combine sliced **Boston lettuce hearts** and quartered heads of **red endive** with **alfalfa sprouts, pea shoots,** and sliced **radishes.**

Combine thickly sliced **Romaine lettuce heart** with **lamb's lettuce,** or **mâche, watercress sprigs, sprouts,** and thinly sliced **scallions.**

Combine small **watercress sprigs, pea shoots, lamb's lettuce,** or **mâche,** inner leaves from a **round green lettuce** with peeled and very finely sliced **cucumber,** adding thinly sliced **scallions.**

Big blowsy lettuces, like **escarole** or other **round green lettuces,** will star on their own. Throw in some crispy **lardons** or **bacon** and sprinkle with sliced **scallions.**

Sprinkle a floppy **round green lettuce** with finely chopped **shallot** and snipped **chives.**

Combine **baby spinach** with thinly sliced **Belgian endive.**

Mix up cresses—**arugula, watercress,** and **mustard and cress** for a punchy peppery salad.

SALAD EXTRAS
raw or cooked beets
coarsely grated carrot
finely sliced radishes
finely sliced cucumber
finely shaved fennel
finely diced red onion
sliced button mushrooms
pomegranate seeds
slivers of apple
avocado
cooked green beans and snow peas
capers
olives
lardons or bacon
quails' eggs

ABOVE LEFT TO RIGHT: *Real French Dressing (see page 194), Caesar (see page 196), and Anchovy and Lemon (see page 195)*

ABOVE LEFT TO RIGHT: *Green Goddess (see page 194) and Sour Cream and Mustard (see page 196)*

ICONIC SALADS

Sausage, egg, and bacon salad

Full breakfast in salad form and, like the Salade Niçoise on page 132, wholly sustaining, great for when you are ravenously hungry. Despite its breakfast inspiration, you need a sausage that is all meat, such as a Toulouse—cooked chorizo would also be good. Equally, explore locally produced sausages of the filler-free variety. As more and more people avoid gluten, these are becoming more readily available.

Serves 4

Salad:
3 eggs
4oz French beans, stalk ends
    trimmed, halved
8 slices unsmoked bacon
1 Romaine lettuce (or similar)
2 tomatoes, cut into wedges
3 cooked sausages, like Toulouse,
    at room temperature, slit in half
    lengthwise, then cut in half

Dressing:
½ teaspoon Dijon mustard
½ teaspoon wholegrain mustard
2 teaspoons red wine vinegar
sea salt and freshly ground black
    pepper
3 tablespoons extra virgin olive oil
3 tablespoons peanut oil

Bring a small saucepan of water to a boil and cook the eggs for 7 minutes, then drain the pan, refill with cold water, and leave them to cool. Bring a second pan of salted water to a boil, add the beans, and cook for 3–4 minutes until just tender. Drain in a sieve, refresh under cold running water, and set aside.

At the same time heat the broiler, and cook the bacon on both sides until golden and crispy. Leave to cool, then cut in half. Discard any tough outer leaves from the lettuce and slice the remaining head into 1-inch strips. Wash, dry, and place in a large bowl. Add the beans, tomatoes, and sausages to the bowl with the lettuce.

To make the dressing, whisk the mustards, vinegar, and some seasoning in a bowl, add the oils, and whisk until the dressing emulsifies into a thin cream. Toss the dressing with the salad ingredients in the bowl. Shell and halve the eggs and gently fold first the bacon and then the eggs into the salad.
Carbohydrate 4.5g Protein 23.4g

Asparagus Russian salad

The asparagus in this salad raises the bar, but you could simply double up on the green beans and sugar snap peas. The essence here is the cocktail of different vegetables cloaked in the comfort of a creamy dressing, with the lively burst of capers and tarragon.

Serves 4

Salad:
14oz celeriac, skin cut off and cut
     into ½-inch dice
a bunch of asparagus, trimmed
4oz fine green beans, topped and
     tailed, and cut into ½-inch dice
4oz sugar snap peas, topped and
     tailed and cut into ½-inch dice
2 tablespoons small capers, (such as
     nonpareille), rinsed, plus a few
     extra to serve
2 teaspoons finely chopped fresh
     tarragon, or 2 tablespoons
     chopped fresh chervil
2 scallions, trimmed and
     finely sliced

Mayonnaise:
½ cup mayonnaise
½ cup sour cream
1 heaping teaspoon Dijon mustard
sea salt
cayenne pepper

Bring two medium saucepans of salted water to a boil. Add the celeriac to one and cook for 7–8 minutes or until just tender. Drain in a colander and set aside to cool.

In the meantime, cut off the asparagus tips and slice the remaining stalks into ½-inch lengths. Add the green beans and asparagus to the second pan, and simmer for 3 minutes, adding the sugar snap peas after 1 minute. Drain everything in a colander and refresh under cold running water, then leave to cool completely.

To assemble the salad, blend the mayonnaise with the sour cream, mustard, and a little salt in a large bowl. Setting aside the asparagus tips, add the remaining green vegetables to the bowl, along with the celeriac, capers, tarragon or chervil, and scallions. Gently stir to combine, then transfer these to a serving dish. Top with the asparagus tips and a few more capers, and dust with a smidgeon of cayenne pepper. Cover and chill until required—unusually, this salad will keep well overnight.

Carbohydrate 7.5g Protein 5.6g

AKA potato salad

Swapping potatoes for celeriac? From our love of celeriac remoulade, we know how good it can be in a salad. This will stand in for a potato salad, with cold roast chicken or shrimp.

Serves 6

Salad:
14oz celeriac, skin cut off and cut
    into ½ inch dice
5oz cherry tomatoes, quartered
1 tablespoon small capers, (such as
    nonpareille), rinsed
4 tablespoons coarsely chopped flat-
    leaf parsley, plus extra to serve

Dressing:
½ cup sour cream
½ cup mayonnaise
1 teaspoon grainy mustard
sea salt
1 tablespoon finely chopped shallot

Bring a medium saucepan of salted water to a boil, add the celeriac, and cook for 7–8 minutes or until just tender. Drain in a colander and set aside to cool.

To make the dressing, blend the sour cream, mayonnaise, and mustard in a large bowl with a little salt. Stir in the shallot, then add the celeriac and gently toss. Reserving a few tomatoes, then mix in the remainder with the capers and parsley. Transfer to a dish or bowl, top with the reserved tomatoes and a little more parsley. The salad can be made several hours in advance, in which case cover and chill until required, removing from the fridge 30 minutes in advance of eating.
Carbohydrate 3.5g Protein 1.9g

Guacamole

Dicing everything by hand takes longer, but the results are a tad more refined. But the speedy route of mixing everything in a food processor is good for dipping and serving as a sauce.

Combine 4oz quartered **cherry tomatoes**, one-eighth of a finely diced **red onion** and 1 teaspoon finely diced **medium-hot red chile** in a bowl, add 2 tablepoons **lime** or **lemon juice**, 2 tablespoons **extra virgin olive oil**, and some **sea salt**, and toss. Spoon in the flesh of 5 **avocados** cut into ½-inch dice and gently toss, then mix in 2 tablespoons coarsely chopped **cilantro**. Try to make this within about 2 hours of serving, before the avocado discolors.
Carbohydrate 2.2g Protein 1.8g (Serves 8)

SPEEDY GUACAMOLE
Omitting the tomatoes, combine the ingredients in a food processor. You can replace the chile with **Tabasco**. You can embellish this by topping with sliced **cherry tomatoes**, a drizzle of **olive oil**, and some chopped **cilantro**.

Frisée and lardons

A whole frisée lettuce is a pleasure to encounter—the inner pale green fronds at the heart go so well with salty lardons and a sharp mustardy vinaigrette. These lettuces can vary enormously in size, so if it's a huge blowsy one, use enough leaves for 4 and reserve the remainder for another salad. Frisées keep well for several days wrapped in a plastic bag in the salad drawer of the fridge.

The best way to prepare a frisée lettuce is to hold it by the stem end and give it a radical trim around the edges, removing many of the dark green leaves, which are tough and too bitter to eat. Now cut out the stem and discard the outside leaves. Separate and tear up the remaining pale green fronds and wash them in a sink of cold water. Shake or spin them dry.

Serves 4

Salad:
4oz fine French beans, topped, tailed and halved
frisée leaves to serve 4
6 large cherry tomatoes, cut into wedges
6oz unsmoked lardons, or diced bacon

Dressing:
1 tablespoon Dijon mustard
2 teaspoons red wine vinegar
sea salt
3 tablespoons peanut oil

Bring a small saucepan of salted water to a boil, add the beans and simmer for 3–4 minutes to leave them firm to the bite. Drain, refresh them in cold water, then toss them into the leaves along with the tomatoes.

To make the dressing, whisk the mustard with the vinegar and some sea salt in a small bowl, then whisk in the oil.

Heat a dry frying pan over medium-low heat and cook the lardons for about 8 minutes, stirring occasionally, until golden. Drain on a double thickness of paper towels. These can be used while warm or at room temperature.

To serve, toss the salad with the dressing, then sprinkle on the lardons.
Carbohydrate 2.2g Protein 8.5g

LOW CARB DESSERTS

So, where do we stand on doughnuts? Out. Meringues? Out. OK, a fruit salad? Actually, only in moderation. As a rule of thumb, the sweeter it tastes, the more carbs it contains. At least more or less, because some fruits are better than others. If you do want to indulge, the ones to go for are berries—raspberries, blackberries, strawberries are all great—and some others—such as melon, kiwi, and plums—are also pretty good, but grapes and bananas are to be avoided.

So the rules here are curious, and if you want to carb-count then it is worth consulting McCance and Widdowson's *The Composition of Foods* (see page 13), which is the best authority on the subject. Pedantic carb-counting is not generally a consideration in this book, the idea being that you can get away with eating as much as you want without worrying, but once we stray into sweet food, all that changes.

Perhaps more poignantly, the guidelines regarding the constantly cited "five-a-day" in relation to how much fruit we should eat are at best confusing and at worst absent. Or, as the nutritionist Dr. Prechtl, who specializes in treating obesity, puts it: "If you eat five portions of fruit a day you are going to put on weight." She suggests aiming for no more than two portions a day, with the remaining three made up of vegetables. Even then, if you actively want to lose weight, simply cut fruit out altogether. Perhaps the best way to regard fruit is as a vegetable with added sugar.

The real importance within your five-a-day is to aim for a variety of colors, which should give you the best range of nutrients.

But back to desserts, and those times when the call comes for something sweet, like a birthday, a weekend treat, or at the end of dinner. What follows are the ones I find the most useful. They are "lower carb," and more or less abide by the rules of plenty of protein, a little fruit, and easy on the fat. The essential thing is that there's chocolate cake, which tastes so decadently rich it is hard to believe just how clean-living it is. I'm not suggesting you live off it, but it's still wildly better than doughnuts.

Very dark and moussey chocolate cake

This cake has all the credentials of a rich chocolate cake. It is indecently gooey with a heady hit of dark chocolate, and you only need the smallest sliver at the end of dinner to feel suitably spoiled. Broken down, however, the "smallest sliver" translates to something like two prunes, a little orange juice, a third of an egg, a fine shaving of butter, and a couple of squares of cocoa-rich chocolate. In short, nothing to beat yourself up about.

The cake can also boast being gluten-free, and it's great for rounding off a special lunch or dinner with a big plate of fruit in attendance, such as one of the suggestions on page 210.

Makes 1 × 8-inch cake
Serves 10

1 cup pitted prunes
¾ cup smooth orange juice
9 tablespoons unsalted butter, diced, plus extra for the pan
7oz dark chocolate (about 85% cocoa), broken into pieces
1 tablespoon dark rum (optional)
6 large eggs, separated
cocoa for dusting

Place the prunes in a small saucepan with half the orange juice and simmer over medium heat, stirring occasionally, until the fruit is sitting in a small amount of sticky syrup. Transfer the prunes and syrup to a food processor and reduce to a thick purée.

Preheat the oven to 350°F and butter an 8-inch cake pan with sides 3 inches deep and a removable bottom. Gently melt the butter and chocolate in a large mixing bowl set over a saucepan with a little simmering water in it. Blend this with the prunes in the food processor (don't worry that initially it will turn very thick), then with the motor running, drizzle in the remaining orange juice, and the rum, if including, at which point the mixture should loosen and become creamy. Transfer it to a large bowl.

Whisk the yolks for a couple of minutes in a medium bowl using an electric mixer until very pale, moussey, and doubled in volume. Fold these into the chocolate mixture in two batches. Now whisk the egg whites until stiff in a large bowl (using clean beaters), fold a third into the mixture to loosen it, and then the remainder in two batches. Pour the mixture into the prepared pan, smooth the surface, and bake for 15 minutes until the cake appears slightly risen around the outside and the surface has set with a glossy sheen; it will remain wet in the center.

Run a knife around the top edge and leave it to cool in the pan, then loosely cover and chill for several hours or overnight. Lightly dust with cocoa just before serving, then remove the pan sides. The cake is delicious either chilled or at room temperature, when it will be soft and mousselike. It will keep for several days and freezes well.
Carbohydrate 13.9g Protein 6.5g

Strawberry and melon cocktail

A summery fruit platter, the loveliest of combinations that takes its inspiration from those kitsch retro cocktail bowls filled with melon balls, not something we tend to have time to prepare these days, or the equipment to make them. But it's a good one to have in the fridge on a summer's day for dipping into, as well as eating after dinner.

Serves 4

¼ Cantaloupe melon, skin and seeds removed, cut into 8 thin segments
2 cups strawberries, hulled and halved unless small, or wild strawberries
2 cups seeded watermelon flesh, cut into ¾-inch dice

Place a couple of slivers of melon on each plate, and top with the strawberries and watermelon.
Carbohydrate 11.9g Protein 1.2g

Orange and passionfruit salad

A good winter fruit salad, which plays on the subtle differences between oranges and clementines. The passionfruit seeds highlight their character. It's lovely for breakfast to kickstart your day as well as at the end of dinner.

Serves 6

1 cup smooth orange juice
a squeeze of lemon juice
3 large oranges
4 clementines
3 passionfruit, halved

Simmer the orange juice in a small saucepan until reduced by half, then pour into a bowl, add a squeeze of lemon juice, and leave to cool.

Using a small sharp (ideally serrated) knife, cut a slice off the top and bottom of each orange, and cut the skin and pith off the sides, exposing the orange flesh. Slice across, ½ inch thick, and remove any seeds. Peel the clementines, cut off and discard a thin slice on the top and bottom, and slice across ½ inch thick. Arrange the fruit slices on a serving plate or in a shallow dish. Pour on the orange juice and spoon on the passionfruit seeds.
Carbohydrate 17g Protein 2.1g

Strawberry mousse

The absence of cream is the making of this mousse. It is as light as air, almost a foam. But the strawberries do need to be seasonally sweet and aromatic; out-of-season berries from countries that grow them solely for export will produce a suitably dull mousse.

Serves 4

2 gelatin sheets, cut into
    broad strips
1 cup apple juice
1⅓ cups strawberries, hulled
½ cup ricotta
½ teaspoon vanilla extract
2 large organic egg whites
1 heaping teaspoon sugar
a few slivers of strawberry or wild
    strawberries, to serve

Place the gelatin in a medium-size bowl, cover with cold water, and leave to soak for 5 minutes, then drain. At the same time simmer the apple juice until it reduces to a quarter of the volume. Pour this into the gelatin and stir to dissolve, then leave for about 5 minutes to cool a little.

Whizz the strawberries with the ricotta and vanilla in a blender, and pass through a sieve into a medium-size bowl. Gradually stir in the gelatin solution. Whisk the whites until stiff in a medium-size bowl using an electric mixer, then sprinkle in the sugar and continue whisking for about 20 seconds until glossy. Fold this, half at a time, into the strawberry base. Divide between four ⅔ cup ramekins or glasses, cover, and chill for half a day or overnight. Serve with a few slivers of strawberry or wild strawberries on top.
Carbohydrate 10.7g Protein 6.8g

Blueberry and apple jello

I love the lively profile of this jello, as sweet as it is tart, and the blueberries and pomegranate seeds both provide their distinct charm. Apple juice will give it a lovely wine-like savor.

Serves 6

5 cups clear apple juice
4 gelatin sheets, cut into broad strips
2 cups blueberries
seeds from 1 pomegranate to serve (optional)

Bring the apple juice to a boil in a medium saucepan and reduce by half. In the meantime, put the gelatin strips in a medium bowl, cover with cold water, and leave to soak for 5 minutes, then drain. Pour the apple juice into the gelatin and stir to dissolve, then leave to cool.

Pour the gelatin solution into a serving bowl, ideally glass, and stir in the blueberries, which will float. Cover and chill for half a day or overnight until set. Serve the jello topped with pomegranate seeds if wished. If you prefer, you can make the jello in 6 individual glasses.
Carbohydrate 23.2g Protein 2g

Jello mess

As refreshing as a long cooling drink at the end of dinner—a stack of easy fruit jellos that are crumbled before being layered with pomegranate seeds.

Serves 6

9 gelatin sheets, cut into broad strips
1¼ cups apple juice
1¼ cups red grape juice
1¼ cups smooth orange juice
3 squeezes of lemon juice
seeds from 2 pomegranates

Divide the gelatin sheets among three medium bowls, cover with cold water, and leave to soak for 5 minutes, then drain them. Pour a couple of tablespoons of boiling water into each batch, and stir to dissolve, then very slowly whisk one juice into each bowl, then add a squeeze of lemon. Cover and chill overnight until set.

Run a fork through each jello flavor to break it up into a soft, crumbly mass, or run a knife through it in a criss-cross pattern to dice it. Divide the apple one among six narrow cup-size glasses, spoon a third of the pomegranate seeds on top, then continue layering with jello and pomegranate seeds, next using the red grape one, and last the orange one. These can be assembled well in advance, in which case cover and chill them.
Carbohydrate 16.2g Protein 4.8g

Crustless mango cheesecake

This cultural concoction is halfway between a German cheesecake and a crustless Sicilian one, taking advantage of mascarpone for richness. I would serve this with the berry sauce, or some raspberries and strawberries.

Makes 1 × 8-inch cheesecake
Serves 10

Cheesecake:
7 tablespoons unsalted butter, melted, plus extra for pan
1 cup smooth orange juice, plus a little for the glaze
10oz mango flesh (from 1½ mangoes)
finely grated zest of 1 lemon
¼ cup sugar
3¼ cups mascarpone
3 large eggs, separated
a pinch of sea salt
1 teaspoon vanilla extract

Top:
1 gelatin sheet, cut into broad strips
4 passionfruit, halved

Preheat the oven to 350°F and butter an 8-inch cake pan with sides 3 inches deep and a removable bottom. Simmer the orange juice in a small saucepan until reduced to a quarter of the volume.

Place the mango in a food processor with the orange juice, lemon zest, and sugar and reduce to a smooth purée, then add the mascarpone, egg yolks, and salt and continue to process until smooth, and finally incorporate the melted butter and vanilla. Press this mixture through a sieve into a large bowl. Whisk the egg whites in another large bowl until stiff using an electric mixer, and fold into the cheesecake mixture in two batches. Transfer this to the prepared pan, smoothing the surface, and bake for 30 minutes until slightly risen and just set. It should still appear loose in the center if you jiggle it from side to side.

Run a knife around the sides of the cheesecake, then return to the turned off oven for 10 minutes, propping the door open using a wooden spoon. Remove and leave to cool completely, setting the pan on a wire rack over a plate or a folded towel—some of the liquid will drain out of the cheesecake, which is completely normal with this type. Don't worry if cracks appear in the center as the passionfruit filling will cover them.

Place the gelatin in a measuring cup, cover with cold water, and soak for 5 minutes, then drain. Pour in 3 tablespoons of boiling water and stir to dissolve. Stir the passionfruit pulp a tablespoon at a time into the gelatin solution; you should have about ⅔ cup, and if not make it up with orange juice. Pour this over the top of the cheesecake within the craterlike rim, then loosely cover with foil and chill for another few hours or overnight. It is best eaten within a day or so.
Carbohydrate 15g Protein 14.2g

WITH A BERRY SAUCE
Process 1 heaping cup hulled **strawberries** and 1⅔ cups **raspberries** with 2 heaping teaspoons of **sugar** and a squeeze of **lemon juice**, and press through a sieve. Serve drizzled over the cheesecake.
Carbohydrate 18.2g Protein 14.6g

Index

Acknowledgments

I did, at the outset, wonder if writing this book might not be seen as part of a cynical business plan. First you write a book about cake, then you write another about how to get rid of the weight. But, I do not know anyone who hasn't at some point in their life had to address a few extra pounds, be it after having a baby or through the slow but steady expansion that comes with age. Understanding how our bodies work and what we can do to reduce our weight, with the minimum of effort and in a way that is sustainable in the long term, can only be of benefit. I wish I had known at the age of 20 what I know today.

I am particularly indebted to Dr. Alexander D. Miras MRCP, PhD, Clinical Lecturer in Metabolic Medicine at Imperial College, London, for his support throughout, and for sharing the results of years of trials and research into the treatment of weight loss. It has turned the book into a collaboration—a meeting of science with a personal passion for cooking and eating well. I am also indebted to Dr. Christina Prechtl, who works alongside Dr. Miras, for approving the copy and sharing her recommendations and guidelines for how to eat.

It was a particular pleasure to have Kyle Cathie in person as Project Editor, ably assisted by Laura Foster. And thanks to the many people at Kyle Books who have also worked away—Julia Barder as Sales and Marketing Director, Nic Jones and David Hearn in Production. Also to Stephanie Evans for copyediting the book, and to Jane Bamforth for proofreading it. Wendy Doyle took on the task of analyzing the nutritional value of all the recipes.

Dan Jones has done a wonderful job of capturing the home-cooked yummy spirit of the dishes, beautifully presented and prepared by the food stylist Annie Rigg, with Wei Tang choosing the tableware and backgrounds. It seems doubly spoiling to also have Sam Wilson's gorgeous line drawings, which are so timeless in the depiction of how we live and eat. Bringing it all together visually, huge thanks to Caroline Clark for her design of the book.

And lastly, I am ever grateful to my agent Lizzy Kremer at David Higham for all her support. And to those immediate members of my family, Jonnie, Rothko, and Louis, who have been starved of potatoes and pasta for the duration, but have continued to use this way of eating to their own advantage.

Published in 2015 by Kyle Books
www.kylebooks.com
general.enquiries@kylebooks.com

Distributed by National Book Network
4501 Forbes Blvd., Suite 200
Lanham, MD 20706
Phone: (800) 462-6420
Fax: (800) 338-4550
customercare@nbnbooks.com

First published in Great Britain in 2014 by Kyle Books, an imprint of Kyle Cathie Ltd.

10 9 8 7 6 5 4 3 2 1

ISBN: 978-1-909487-20-8

Text © 2014 Annie Bell
Design © 2014 Kyle Books
Photography © 2014 Dan Jones
Illustrations © 2014 Sam Wilson

Project Editor: Kyle Cathie
Editorial Assistant: Laura Foster
Copy Editor: Stephanie Evans
Proofreader: Jane Bamforth
Designer: Caroline Clark
Photographer: Dan Jones
Illustrator: Sam Wilson
Nutritionist: Wendy Doyle
Food Stylist: Annie Rigg
Prop Stylist: Wei Tang
Production: Nic Jones and David Hearn

Please note all recipe analysis is per portion.

Library of Congress Control No. 2014945513

Color reproduction by ALTA London.
Printed and bound in China by C&C Offset Printing Company Ltd.